KANSAS
ODDITIES

ROGER L. RINGER

KANSAS ODDITIES

JUST BILL THE ACTING ROOSTER
THE LOCUST PLAGUES OF GRASSHOPPER FALLS
NATURALIST CAMPS
— and MORE —

Foreword by MARCI PENNER

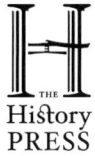

Published by The History Press
Charleston, SC
www.historypress.com

Copyright © 2018 by Roger L. Ringer
All rights reserved

Cover images: Albin Longren in airplane. *Courtesy of Kansas State Historical Society*; binding wheat in Sedgwick County. *Courtesy of Wichita-Sedgwick County Historical Museum.*

First published 2018

Manufactured in the United States

ISBN 9781467139229

Library of Congress Control Number: 2018932101

Notice: The information in this book is true and complete to the best of our knowledge. It is offered without guarantee on the part of the author or The History Press. The author and The History Press disclaim all liability in connection with the use of this book.

All rights reserved. No part of this book may be reproduced or transmitted in any form whatsoever without prior written permission from the publisher except in the case of brief quotations embodied in critical articles and reviews.

*Many books do a short dedication to someone special. There are so many inspirations and people in my life that I would like to dedicate this to, but it would go on for too many pages. So, I will follow with a few special ones.
In memory of Daniel Ringer, Lloyd Ringer, K.O. Huff, Carl Becker, Duane Nelson and Prairie Dog Dave Lafferty. Also to the teachers who fired my imagination and love for history: Mr. Dale Churchman and Milton Mathews of Goddard High School, as well as Mrs. Crook, who suffered my English.
My family—mom, Charlotte, and father, Ronald, plus my brother, Rodney—who have put up with the project and been very supportive, as well as a group of historians, journalists and Kansans who continue to inspire me: Beccy Tanner, Marci Penner, Martha Farrell, Dr. Jim Hoy, Bill Ellington, Dr. Don Coldsmith, Amy Bickel and the Honorable Patsy Terrell.
This work would not have been possible without the patience and work of Mary Brohammer.
And to all the Kansans who look past convention, think outside the box and make Kansas an interesting place to live.*

CONTENTS

Foreword, by Marci Penner	9
Acknowledgements	11
Kansas Oddities	13
Bibliography	135
Index	161
About the Author	175

FOREWORD

Roger Ringer loves being a Kansan and thrives on digging up the obscure, the quirky and the fascinating. Kansas is a state that needs assistance in revealing itself, and Roger obliges. From functional inventions and interesting people to tragedies and legends, you'll learn many of the things not usually noted in Kansas history journals.

For instance, did you know the hassock was manufactured in Cawker City? The world's largest ball of sisal twine has dominated our thoughts of Cawker City until Roger dug up this business success story. He'll relate how George Barnett and his son, E.J., invented a stowaway footrest made of plastic and how some designs even stored General Electric and Eureka canister vacuum cleaners.

Short, easy-to-read essays will open your eyes to such people as Jacob Haynes, who came up with the clothesline tightener, and Jacob Wiens Buller, who invented the snap coupler hitch. The history of the automatic telephone exchange is personalized with a story about two undertakers. One was getting all the business because his girlfriend, a telephone operator, was directing all the business to him! This practice led to the automatic exchange.

Roger did the hard work of digging up the "rest of the story," so you can sit back and enjoy these accounts of little-known but interesting Kansas history.

Marci Penner, Director,
Kansas Sampler Foundation

ACKNOWLEDGEMENTS

There have been a huge number of people who assisted with the research for these stories, including museums, libraries, city clerks, local historians, family members, friends and acquaintances—on various subjects. There are too many to be able to list. Many stories are due to small snippets that I and others were able to find on stories that have slipped through the main history of our state. Also, thanks to all the people over the years who encouraged me to write down these obscure stories that I heard about in my travels around Kansas. I am in your debt.

KANSAS ODDITIES

THE ARKANSAS RIVER

Let's get something straight: anywhere native Kansans go, they give themselves away when the topic is the Arkansas River. You will find them very fervent over the proper way to pronounce it. Many out-of-state people laugh over the stubborn way we cling to the pronunciation of the river as the "Ar*kansas*." There is no *w* on the end of the name.

The 1820 map of America—of what would become the United States—shows the 1819 "Arkansaw" Territory. At that time, what would become the major part of Oklahoma was part of the Arkansaw Territory, the Red River being the boundary with Mexico. There had been a dispute over the pronunciation of Arkansaw up until the 1880 quarrel between two state senators in Arkansas, one wanting a Spanish pronunciation and the other a French pronunciation, where the *s* remains silent.

It is accepted that *Kansas* is based on the Kanza Indians. The Kanzas, whose name means "the people of the south wind," belonged to the Siouan linguistic stock. The Osage, Quapaw, Omaha and Ponca groups are a part of a distinct subgroup called Dheigiha, according to Dr. J.O. Dorsey in 1897.

The French "Arkansaw," meaning "downstream place," was interpreted from the Sioux word *acansa*. This was the basis for the naming of Arkansas. It is fitting that Arkansas decided to have a different pronunciation between the two states. They can do what they want with their own state. However, the actions of the Arkansas legislature have no binding action outside its own state. It's the only state that needed to legislate the proper pronunciation of its name—here is where a lot of jokes start. If it wants to rewrite history, that is fine. However, upstream we will be happy to pronounce the Ar*kansas* River properly. We just never figured out why the Coloradans bought into it. After all, they were originally part of the Kansas Territory.

THE FIRST BUFFALO BILL

Before Buffalo Bill Cody, there was Buffalo Bill (William) Mathewson. In fact, William Cody worked for Mathewson for a while when he was young at his trading ranch near the Great Bend of the Arkansas River. Of Scottish descent, Mathewson was a contemporary of Kit Carson's. Mathewson hunted, traded and trapped across the plains, and in 1858, he created the Cow Creek Ranch near the Great Bend of the Arkansas River. Always a quiet man, he became a legend in the eyes of both the Plains Indians and white men.

Chief Satanta of the Kiowa tribe tried to take goods from the trading post without paying for them. Satanta was an exceptionally tall Indian for the time and a perfect physical specimen. Bill proceeded to give Satanta a tremendous thrashing and kicked him and his companions out of the store. The incident made him famous, and the Kiowas named him "Sillpah Sinpahor," or "Long Beard Dangerous Man." The incident made lifelong friends of Satanta and Bill.

When the Kiowas went on the warpath, Satanta rode hundreds of miles to warn Bill. On June 20, 21 and 22, 1860, Bill and five employees held off a superior force of attackers. As a freight train was coming down the Santa Fe Trail, the Indians turned from attacking the trading post to intercepting the freight train. The column was lightly armed and did not know that its cargo contained large quantities of firearms, powder and shot. Bill armed himself to the teeth and, in a scene that could have been in a John Wayne movie, single-handedly rode through the attackers, firing as he went, and made it to the freighters to warn them and inform them of the cargo. With the freight's arms and munitions unboxed, they fought off the attack.

Bill earned the name of "Buffalo Bill" during a time of drought and famine. He shot buffalo and sent carcasses to settlements in the eastern part of the territory, saving many people from starvation. Bill scouted for General

Blunt's expedition and did much to bring the tribes together for the Little Arkansas Treaty. This preceded the great Medicine Lodge Treaty. When he was scouting, Bill would go out to villages, which was dangerous work. He made a practice of sneaking up on the villages and just appearing.

In his lifetime, he was responsible for returning no fewer than fifty-four women and children captives. In Wichita, he led the effort to find and return little Rea Woodman, age five. A group of "pants" Indians had been camping near Wichita, and when they moved south, Rea was missing. It was feared that the Indians had kidnapped her—she had actually gone into a tepee and fallen asleep. She was simply packed up with everything else as they left.

A posse was formed to go after the Indians. Wisely, Bill took Rea's father and one other man and went ahead of the posse. Circling around the group, which were now camped on the Cowskin Creek fishing, the trio rode in from the south so they would not be suspicious of them. They sat around the fire and smoked and talked. In the conversation, Bill brought up their possibility of doing some trading. When asked if the Indians had anything they wanted to trade, they brought out Rea. They knew that being found with the girl could have brought a lot of trouble on them.

In his best trading style, Bill hem-hawed a bit and said that she was so little she would only be worth fifty cents to him. Looking at Rea's father, he caught the line and offered a pocketknife. They took their trade and left the Indians peacefully behind, taking Rea with them. By his cool acting, Bill averted what would have been a bloodbath if the posse had just ridden in to take Rea back. Whenever Rea would act up a little, her dad would say, "I sure miss that pocketknife."

Bill was an early resident of Wichita, and everyone looked up to him. His pasture became the camping ground for newcomers as well as the site of rodeos and fairs. It was the location of the first Joyland. Buffalo Bill Cody would come and visit him at his home. When times were lean, Bill had to sell his favorite buffalo rifle. It is said that Cody bought the gun and returned it to him.

STAFFORD COUNTY SHORT NOTES

Inventor on the plains, "Doc" Jacob Haynes designed a clothesline lightener, manufactured on the farm for a time. He hired a group of itinerant Italians and put them on the road as peddlers. Doc stocked their wagons and later automobiles with pins, needles, buttons, lace and all manner of necessities and sent them door to door all over the country. Children of the time remember going to the Haynes place to buy the summer supply of fish hooks and line.

Doc would require his men to leave their watches at the house when they came to work in the mornings and pick them up on the way home. Doc would tell them when it was time to eat and go home. There were no clock watchers in his employ.

Doc Haynes was never a practicing doctor but rather an entrepreneur always looking for a way to get rich. He built a hatchery and shipped White Leghorn chicks and eggs all over the country from the Macksville Depot.

One story told throughout the years holds that a dugout on the bank of the Rattlesnake Creek to the west of the Searles homestead was used by the Dalton Gang as a layover stop to rest and water their horses. They would follow the creek southwest toward Meade, originally known as Meade Center.

Charles Grim always planted cane for making syrup. The syrup was cooked in a large iron pot over a fire, and it had to be stirred constantly. The community gathered to help. The men stirred, the women sat on the ground and talked and the kids played. Everyone had a good time. In later years the press used a horse or mule to press out the juice.

Information in this section courtesy of the Stafford County Historical Museum.

JUST BILL: OUT OF THE FRYING PAN AND INTO THE MOVIES

One of Stafford County's most famous residents was a White Plymouth Rock rooster named Just Bill. Bill was bred and raised in Lexington, Nebraska, by C.W. Winkler and sold in 1946 for $100 to Earl H. Kelly (1893–1956) of Stafford County.

Kelly was a private detective, retired farmer and oil man who exhibited livestock and poultry successfully for more than forty years. Poultry raising was a hobby to keep him from "going crazy" between rounds of wheat tending.

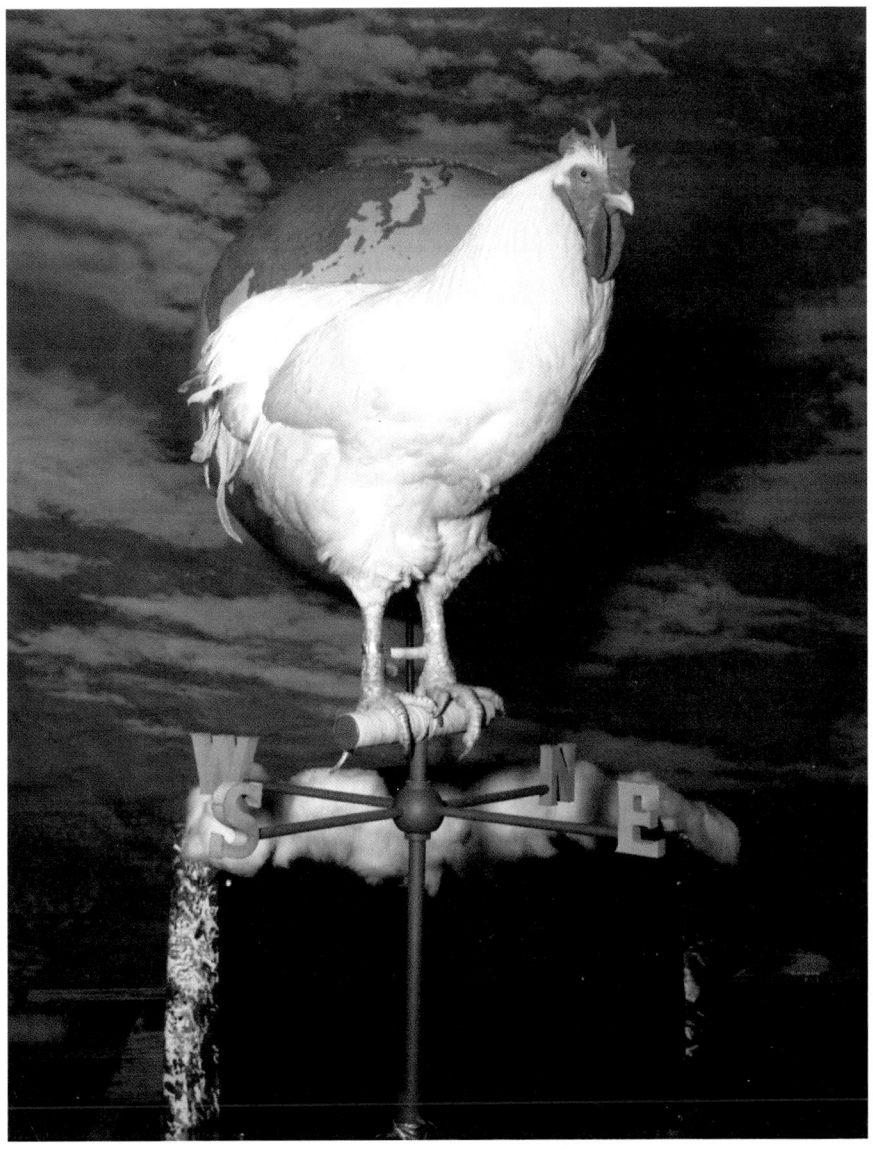

Just Bill, the rooster that broke into the movies. *Courtesy of Stafford County Historical Museum.*

According to *Poultry Press* (March 1947), at a poultry exhibition in Fort Worth, Texas, "Bill was acclaimed as one of the greatest specimens of the breed ever produced." Kelly entered Bill in a grand champion rooster show at the Oklahoma State Fair, sponsored by the movie studio RKO.

Bill won out over hundreds of competitors from forty states. Actor Wayne Morris was one of the judges.

Bill came through with flying colors to become the Charles Atlas of all barnyard fowl. After Bill's victory, the owner was presented with a large trophy and a fat movie contract. Bill became the RKO trademark rooster, crowing in the Warner-Pathé newsreels that played in theaters before movies.

A 1947 issue of the *Stafford Courier* reported, "A White Rock rooster owned by Earl Kelly is breaking into the movies. He's a natural champion and conducts himself like one in front of poultry breeders, photographers, and reporters. Bill crows when a rooster should crow and does it so well he is to be the rooster used as the trademark in the Warner-Pathé news reel. At the request of the show management and photographers, Kelly remained with Bill in Oklahoma a couple of days after the show ended, for picture taking."

Another story noted, "The rooster goes to Hollywood next week for more movie work. Kelly was offered the trip but says 'he got enough of the high-powered photographer's lights at Oklahoma City. A friend of his in Hollywood is a poultry man and will take care of Bill while the bird is there.'"

As Bill was on his way to Hollywood, Kelly was quoted in the *Corpus Christi Caller* of December 10, 1947, as saying affectionately, "He doesn't crow often, but when he does, all hell breaks loose! I sure hate to see him go; we've been through a lot together."

Bill became so valuable that Kelly insured him for $1,000 with Lloyd's of London. He garnered many accolades during his illustrious career. He and Kelly appeared in *LIFE* magazine. His photo graced the covers of *Southwest Poultryman* (January 1948) and the *American Poultryman* (March 1952). His story appeared in newspapers all over, including the *Daily Oklahoman, Long Beach Independent, Denver Post, Dayton News, Poultry News* (PA), *Tulsa Tribune, Evening World* (Omaha) and the *Corpus Christi Caller*, among others.

Newspaper and magazine clippings, photographs and awards chronicling Bill's career were preserved in a scrapbook by Mrs. Earl (Nell O'Conner) Kelly (1894–1980). The scrapbook was donated to the Stafford County Museum in 1990 by Jane Helmer (Mrs. Kelly's niece).

Story information courtesy of Stafford County Museum director (and author) Michael Hathaway.

EXODUSTERS

Kansas was engaged in the Civil War long before the guns were fired on Fort Sumter. The battles for a territory becoming a free or slave state were a precursor to what would happen. Kansas became an important part of helping slaves escape from the chains and labors of that horrid institution.

Following the end of the Civil War, there was a mass migration of freed slaves from the South. A story was spread that the government had set aside land for former slaves. The story was not true, but it did start a migration movement.

From Kansas came John Brown, who took up the cause of the slave and attempted to spark a revolution to end slavery. Kansas was known for abolitionist free thinkers. They were inspired and led by Benjamin "Pap" Singleton, a former slave from Tennessee.

When the Civil War broke out, black men of the First Colored Infantry were the first black units to go into the U.S. Army and the first to fight. Kansas was "the promised land." While most Kansans know the story of Nicodemus and the settlement of former slaves in that area, what is not known is that some other settlements were successful in Stafford and Barton Counties as well.

In Stafford County, Ohio Township—near the former town of Zion Valley (named for a group of Mormon settlers), now named St. John after Governor John St. John—there was a settlement of Exodusters. They settled on Sections 6, 14, 17, 20 and 30 and established a cemetery. Martin Black Cemetery was named for a family of black settlers in the area by that name. These settlers were members of the Baptist church and the African Episcopal church located in St. John. The numbers peaked in 1914 at 400 to 425. Family names included Scott, Martin, Jifford, Davis, Thomas, Glass, Bowen, Roberts, Rogers, Gossip, Embry, Gracey, Kendall, Fuller, Minnis, Walden and Tyler. A noted member of the community was Elsie Scott, who became a Chicago educator. She maintained a modest home in St. John until her death.

Railroad flyers may have attracted a large number of settlers to Ohio Township, but the sandy soils, wildlife, creeks and streams proved to be good landing for homesteading.

Several Exodusters were buried at the Eden Valley Cemetery. George Washington Walker purchased a quarter-section of land near what is now Seward. Soon several families joined him as neighbors. One of these neighbors was Oscar Micheaux, who became the first black movie producer.

The Micheauxes moved to the area in the early 1890s. Oscar's grandmother Melvina and Aunt Harriet Robinson are buried in Eden Valley.

Oscar Micheaux made forty-three movies from 1919 to 1948 and is considered one of the most prolific black movie producers of all time. In 2010, the U.S. Postal Service issued a commemorative stamp with his image. When Oscar died in 1951, he was buried at the Great Bend Cemetery in an unmarked grave for four decades. In the 1980s and 1990s, local historians, film buffs and Hollywood celebrities began researching his life. Fans including Spike Lee, Robert Townsend, Ruby Dee and Ossie Davis purchased a headstone to honor him.

The Barton County Arts Council, located in Great Bend, showcases art and artists and has an exhibit recognizing the spirit of the Exodusters movement. In 1890, the black population of Kansas was slightly more than sixteen thousand; by 1980, the numbers were closer to forty thousand.

Near Beeler, in western Kansas, is the area that George Washington Carver homesteaded during the mid-1880s.

LOCUST PLAGUE: GRASSHOPPER FALLS

In February 1854, not long after the opening of Kansas as a territory, a man named Henry Zen located near the falls on the Grasshopper River. On Christmas Day 1854, James Frazer, Robert Riddle, Hozea Jolly and Andrew J. Whitney staked out a settlement. In the spring of 1855, Isaac Cody (Buffalo Bill's father) surveyed the town site of Grasshopper Falls. One hundred maps were sent back east to advertise the town.

The town is known today as Valley Falls, and the river is known as the Delaware. It is located above Perry Reservoir and north and east of Topeka. The falls were a natural site for the mill that was built there. The town today is a pleasant town with tree-lined streets, schools, churches, a large parkland, a swimming pool and sixty businesses. But why did they change the town's name?

Over the years, Grasshopper Falls fell victim to a number of disasters, including fires and multiple grasshopper plagues. Grasshopper infestations occurred in the region in 1820 and again in 1855, 1860 and 1861. The worst grasshopper plague occurred in 1874. The people were so fed up with the recurring hopper plagues that in 1875 they asked the Kansas legislature to change the name of the township, river and town, thus becoming the

Delaware River and Valley Falls. But even the Garden of Eden can become embroiled in controversy, and even such a pleasant place can fall victim to a swell in intolerant thought and action.

CASTLETON MOVIE SET

Castleton was platted out as a stage stop by C.C. Hutchinson in 1872. The town was named after Mr. Hutchinson's new bride's hometown, Castleton, Vermont. Today, it is listed as a "ghost town," but there are still several residents who are alive and well there. The rural community in Reno County is northeast of Pretty Prairie, or two miles west of Highway K-14 (previously K-17) north of the North Fork of the Ninnescah River.

The town had a red brick Santa Fe Railroad depot that caught the attention of a producer in Hollywood. The 20th Century Fox movie company moved in and built a set around the depot and the post office. It built a fire station, barbershop, livery stable and other props and turned Castleton into Sevillious, Illinois, circa 1895. Starring Jean Peters and David Wayne, the movie *Wait 'til the Sun Shines, Nellie* was shot there.

The film was released in July 1952, and the world premiere was in Hutchinson, Kansas, on May 14, 1952. Many locals were used in the movie, and it created a lot of excitement. A local seamstress named Mrs. Grillot was hired to fit all the costumes for the extras, which were stored at the high school. The story was based on the book *I Hear Them Sing* by Fredrick Reyher.

Kansas has seen a lot of filmmaking over the years. The attractive period settings in many towns and the helpfulness and friendliness of the people have always made Kansas a great place to film. Today, the red brick depot that attracted the film crew to town has been razed, and the post office building was moved to Great Bend, where it can be seen at the local historical museum. There may have been an original building or two in the background during filming of the movie, but a lot of the town has been razed or abandoned.

The song "Wait 'til the Sun Shines, Nellie" was a popular tune written in 1905 by Harry Von Tilzer, with lyrics by Andrew B. Sterling. Traditionally, the floor traders on the New York Stock Exchange sing the song on the last day of the year and on Christmas Eve. It remains a popular tune for barbershop groups.

SKYSCRAPERS OF THE PLAINS

Kansas is wheat country. The face of the prairie was changed with the introduction of Turkey Red wheat, brought in by the Mennonite immigrants who raised it in Russia in the area known as the Ukraine. The first Turkey Red was planted near Goessel in Marion County.

As the practice of raising wheat spread throughout the state, structures were needed to store the grain and terminals to route the grain through to the various mills and markets, as well as for export. The first structures were wooden elevators, many covered in sheet metal. But as the size of farms grew and the equipment to raise and harvest crops improved, the old structures proved to be too small. Plus, they were more subject to fire and wind damage.

A new technique called slip-form construction allowed concrete to be continuously poured, and the white elevators we are familiar with today were built. Predominant in the design and construction of these "skyscrapers of the plains" was a partnership formed in 1926 between Clint Chalmers and John Borton. Chalmers and Borton, headquartered in Hutchinson, Kansas, built 80 percent of the concrete elevators, and many are still in use today.

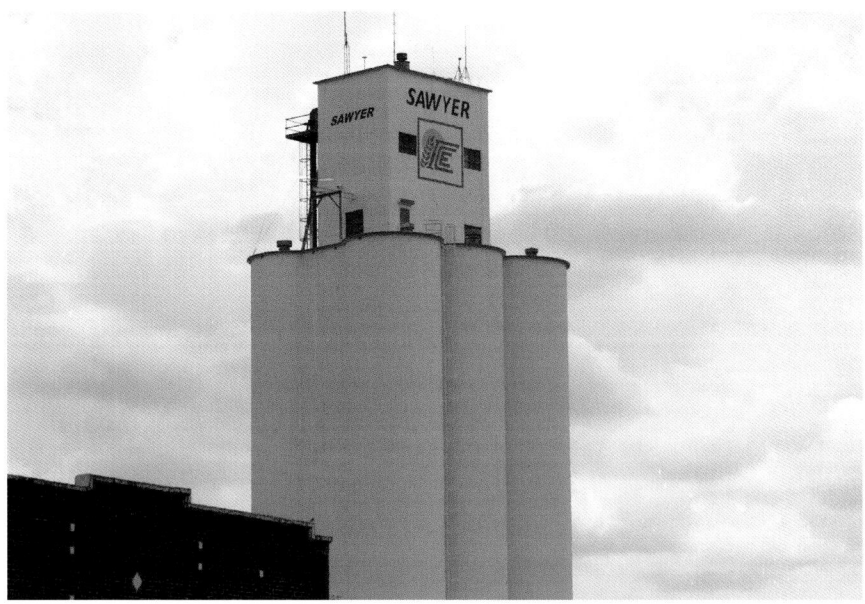

Coop grain elevator, Sawyer, Kansas. *Photo by Roger Ringer.*

The company built three thousand elevators in seventeen states. In 1958, it built a $22 million terminal elevator that became the world's largest. After Chalmers retired, the company was solely owned and was renamed Borton. Today, Borton LLC is owned by a group of Wichita investors—Jim Tadtman, Jim Snook and Sherwood Construction. It builds all forms of slip-form concrete structures. Other companies that built concrete elevators included Tillatson, Mayer-Osborn and Johnson-Simpson.

Many of these structures are now more than fifty years old, and many are still giving good service to the farmer. As the increase in bushels per acre and demand worldwide grows, demand for larger elevators is increasing. Some older structures are being rebuilt or taken down and replaced with new structures. Also, new structures are being added to some of the old elevators, and the original structures are being remodeled and updated.

As a side note, Kansas State University is the only university that has a degree program in milling science technology. The world comes to Kansas for education and the latest technology.

THRESHING MACHINE CANYON

The location of the Bluffton Station on the Butterfield Overland route on the Smoky Hill Trail has a unique history. The name Threshing Machine Canyon is a result of an Indian attack that occurred in 1867. The area near the station had high bluffs, and for years, travelers on the trail would carve their names on the sides of the canyon walls.

In 1867, a threshing machine (possibly two) was being transported by freighters. Common reports say that the threshing machine was being delivered to Brigham Young at Salt Lake City, Utah. There is no record found that the church was the intended recipient as the result of an order placed by Brigham Young or anyone connected to the Church.

The freighters who were traveling the trail decided to camp too close to the canyon walls, making them vulnerable to attack by Indians. There is no evidence of any survivors of the attack, and the threshing machine was burned. The station was moved farther away from the vulnerable area. The Smoky Hill Trail was a major artery to the Denver and Rocky Mountain areas. Due to the amount of material and people traveling the trail, it was a very important part of the Cherry Creek Gold Rush history. In fact, the Smoky Hill Trail is very close to the path taken by the later Interstate 70.

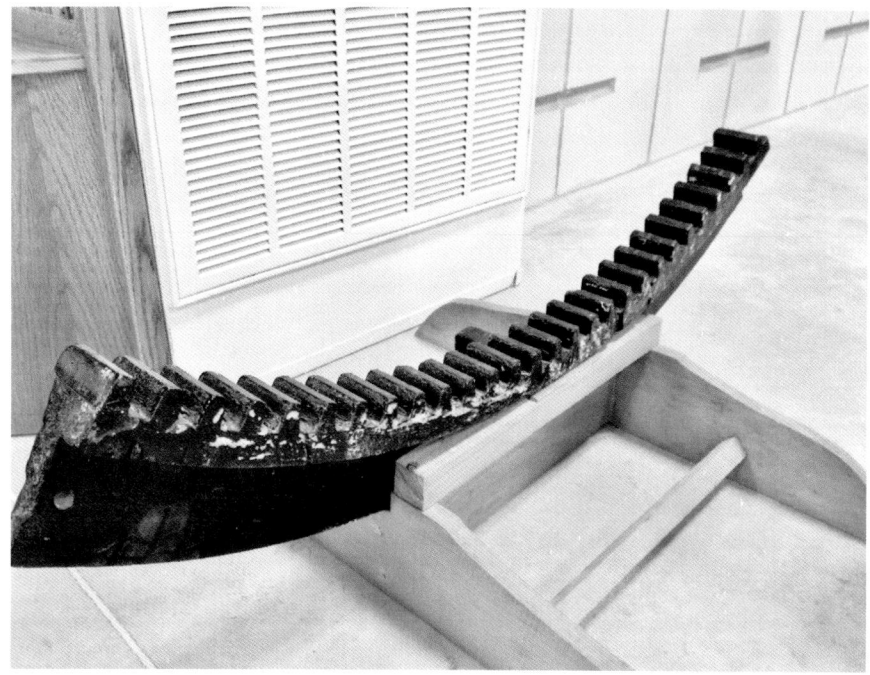

Gear from burnt threshing machine from Threshing Machine Canyon. *Courtesy of Trego County Historical Museum.*

The remains of the threshing machine stayed at the site, and for many years, travelers picked up pieces as souvenirs. What ultimately remained at the site is now in the Trego County Historical Museum in Wakeeney. There are no identifying marks on the remaining pieces to identify what brand the threshing machine was.

The canyon is near the town of Bluffton, but the actual site is now underwater due to the building of the Cedar Bluffs Reservoir. Some of the carvings on the bluff walls can be seen in the wildlife area. This area is closed during different seasons. If you want to visit the site, it is good idea to stop at the State Park Office for information.

Threshing Machine Canyon is an interesting and a violent part of the history of Kansas. The story of the Indian raids during 1867 resulted in the recall of George Armstrong Custer from enforced leave after his court-martial. The Winter Campaign resulted in the attack on Black Kettle's camp on the Washita River in Oklahoma Territory.

SELLERS MOTOR CAR COMPANY

Between 1909 and 1912, Hutchinson, Kansas, had the Sellers Motor Car Company, located at 705 South Main. The company was originally named the St. Joe Motor Company in Elkhart, Indiana, before the company was purchased and moved to Hutchinson. There were several prototypes that were designed by the company and never built, but the main model was the Sellers 35. The Sellers 35 was a high-quality automobile with four cylinders that was rated at thirty-five horsepower. It had a full floating rear axle. One of the features used to sell the car was its inability to "grind" gears in the transmission. In a newspaper ad, the number of automobiles sold each week ran from three to ten. An active sales force was put into the field, and many inquiries came in from potential dealers for the Sellers.

In the first automobile races run at the state fairgrounds on the half-mile track, the Sellers, driven by Harry Shoemaker, ran head to head with George C. Wiles, who was racing an EMF automobile. The track was used after all the horse races were run. Shoemaker, who was the original designer of the Sellers, came in second. These were two-lap, four-lap and ten-lap free-for-all races. Under a threatening sky, the events turned out six thousand people.

Shoemaker was the designer and managed the factory. On file is a patent granted to Harry for a Motor Tractor. One-third each was assigned to Shoemaker, Sellers and a John H. Greider from Freeport, Illinois. The patent was filed in November 1910 and issued in 1911. To date, there is no evidence of the tractor being built by Sellers or any other company. At some point, the patent may have been transferred, but no evidence has been found that any tractor was ever produced.

A Sellers advertisement claimed that the factory had twenty thousand square feet of space. It goes on to say that the factory had twenty-five to thirty power machines that produced more than two hundred parts on-site for its autos. The steel for the transmissions was said to be German Krupp steel, considered the best that money could buy. The Sellers touring car had a wheel base of 112 inches.

William Newlin was listed as the vice-president and manager of the company. The secretary and treasurer was A. Pearson. The company motto was, "There is no waiting period for repairs of the Sellers Motor Car." The factory offered immediate repair on site should anything go wrong.

The Sellers Motor Car Company was entirely locally owned and financed. The total number of Sellers cars produced is not known, but the top number

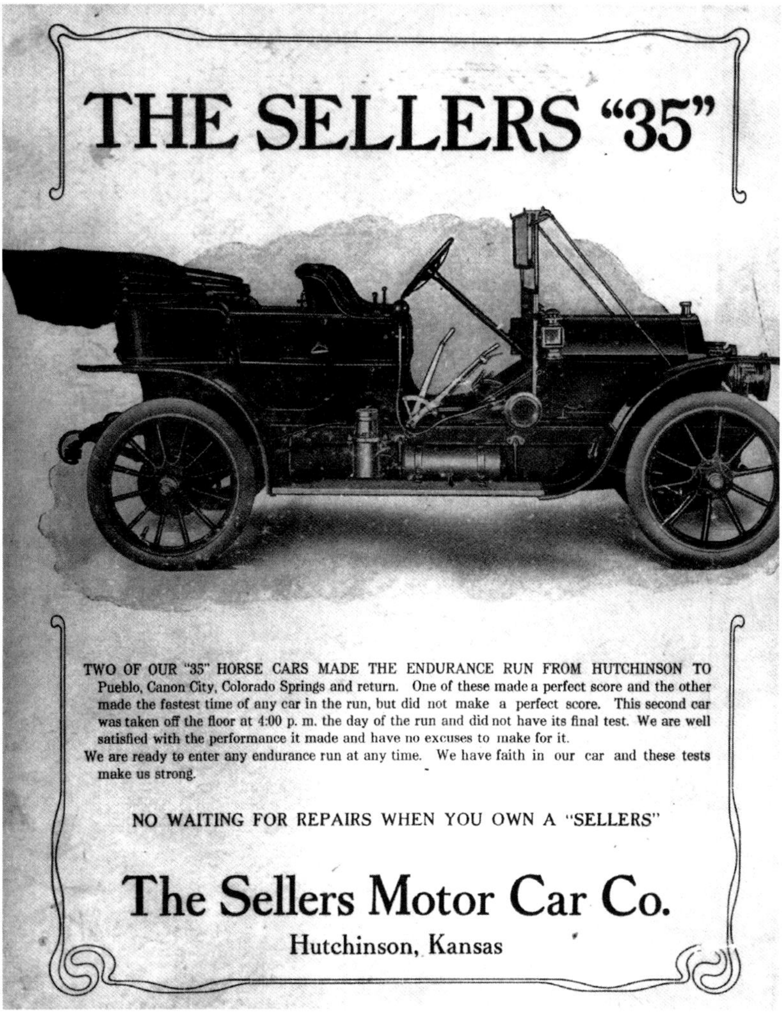

THE SELLERS "35"

TWO OF OUR "35" HORSE CARS MADE THE ENDURANCE RUN FROM HUTCHINSON TO Pueblo, Canon City, Colorado Springs and return. One of these made a perfect score and the other made the fastest time of any car in the run, but did not make a perfect score. This second car was taken off the floor at 4:00 p. m. the day of the run and did not have its final test. We are well satisfied with the performance it made and have no excuses to make for it.

We are ready to enter any endurance run at any time. We have faith in our car and these tests make us strong.

NO WAITING FOR REPAIRS WHEN YOU OWN A "SELLERS"

The Sellers Motor Car Co.
Hutchinson, Kansas

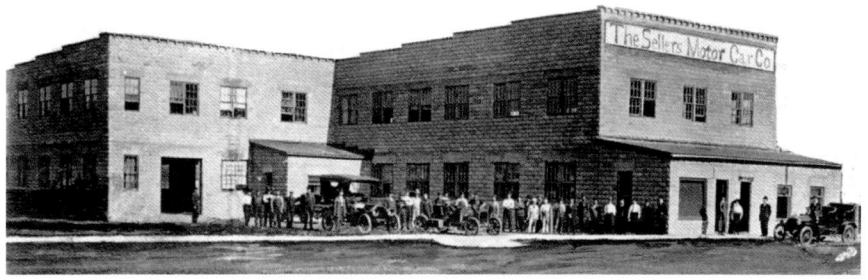

Kansas Oddities

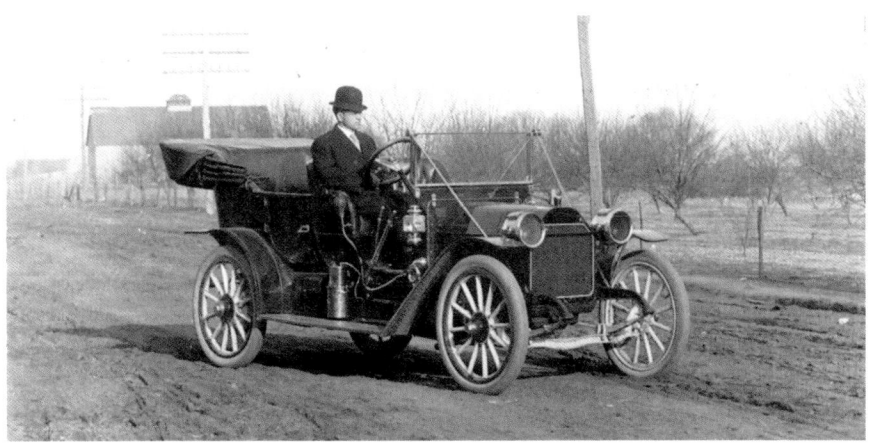

Above: Sellers 35 automobile; *Opposite, top*: Sellers 35 advertisement; *Opposite, bottom*: Sellers Automobile factory in Hutchinson, Kansas, circa 1904. *Courtesy of Reno County Historical Museum.*

for 1909–12 would probably not exceed three hundred. There are several pictures of the Sellers Motor Cars owned by the Kansas Historical Society and the Reno County Museum.

The Sellers had the same problem that others had trying to manufacture and sell motor cars as well as tractors: competition from the East and availability of materials. The population density and competition caused prices to be too high to compete. The company went broke, and all investors lost money on the company, bankrupting several.

ENGINE 252: ORIENT RAILROAD

The Orient Railroad, formally known as the Kansas City, Mexico & Orient Railroad, was chartered with the intentions of connecting the Midwest southward through Mexico to the port of Topolobampo, Sinaloa, Mexico. The United States' portion of the railway was incorporated in 1900. This part was completed from Wichita to Alpine, Texas. Grading took place from El Dorado to Bazaar, Kansas. The original Primary Shops were located in Fairview, Oklahoma, but burned down in 1910. The shop was reestablished in Wichita. The company was bankrupt in 1912, but the receiver, William T. Kemper, reorganized it into the KCM&O Railroad. Reorganized again in 1925, the railroad took back its original name and was referred to as the Orient Railroad.

As near as the research can tell, Engine nos. 251, 252 and 253 were part of a purchase in 1903 from the Luco Works in Schenectady, New York. The fascination with Engine no. 252 stems from an article in the "Tihen Notes" of the *Wichita Beacon*. The story synopsis was that Engine no. 252 was being rebuilt after Pancho Villa had derailed it during the Mexican Revolution.

From research, it seems a possibility that Engine no. 252 and its counterparts could have been a group purchase from what is known as the "Russian Engines." Those engines were part of an order built for the Tsar Nicholas of Russia. They were never delivered, however, when the Bolshevik Revolution toppled the government of the tsar and the Communists took power. The Baldwin 2-210-0s were sold to various railroads around the nation, including the Orient.

From various reports, it seems that these were probably not the Russian engines but the Luco Works engines. The story is that while operating in Mexico during the revolution, Pancho Villa's rebels attacked the train. This was a large combination passenger/freight train being pulled by Engine nos. 251, 252 and 253. The trestle over which it ran was fired, and the engines and the train were run into the flames and derailed into the bottom of a large gully, where they rested for three years. The new trestle was built around the original wreckage. The Mexican railroad came out and raised Engine nos. 251 and 252 and took them to the Mexican shops, where they were renovated and put back in service. Presumably Engine no. 253 is still in the gully.

After some time, the Orient went into receivership, and the Santa Fe Railroad purchased the company. For some reason, Engine no. 252 was returned to Wichita and taken to the Santa Fe shops, rebuilt again and put back into service. The engine was changed from a wood burner to a coal burner but retained the diamond smokestack that was its trademark.

The numbering that the Santa Fe put on the old 252 engine is unknown, but it spent the rest of its service life in the Southern Division of the Santa Fe Railroad in Oklahoma and Texas. It is unknown when it was taken out of service or its disposition. Since the diesel electric engines were coming into service during World War II, it is reasonable to suspect that the engine was scrapped for the war effort.

The Mexican section of the Orient Railroad became the predecessor of the modern Mexican railroad today. The dream of rail service from the Midwest to the Pacific Ocean, connecting to the Orient markets, never became a reality, but the AT&SF made those connections through California.

RICHARDSON MANUFACTURING

One of the major economic factors in the Cawker City area has been the Richardson Manufacturing Company. Over the years, the company has been a major employer and an integral part of the community. The company was founded by a farm boy who loved to tinker and spent his free time on the farm in the workshop, building things that made life and farming easier.

Emmit David Richardson was born in 1881 south of Glen Elder, on Walnut Creek. His father had come to Mitchell County and purchased 320 acres of land. The family was one of the earliest settlers in the area. Emmit, the firstborn, was later joined by his brother, Russell. Being taught at home by his mother, Mary, as they were too far from school, Emmit excelled in math even before he was formally enrolled in school. In 1890, his mother died, and Emmit took on many of the jobs on the farm.

It was not long before Emmit's inventiveness began to show. He would spend every spare moment with the forge and piles of scrap that he would form into useful things. While attending school, he helped his father on the farm. Eventually, his father remarried, and an additional two sisters and brother were born. An excellent student, Emmit went to high school at Glen Elder and became interested in electricity as well as mechanical subjects. He built a miniature traction engine that would be the forerunner of a full-sized project when he attended college.

Emmit went to Kansas State Agricultural College and there saw his first automobile. He ordered a set of engine castings and had soon made his own engine, building an automobile from gears and the engine of an old John Deere binder. It is thought that his automobile was the second in Mitchell County when he drove home for the first time in 1903. The top speed was 12.5 miles per hour, and the 105-mile trip took two days.

In order to pay for his education, he decided to form a threshing crew and was able to purchase a Huber steam engine and an Advance separator. Using the income from threshing wheat, it took him six years to graduate. During his time in college, he made himself useful by fabricating tools and an electric motor for the machine shop. He also worked on the janitorial staff at the college farm. During his third year, he built his own engineer's transit and used it to survey streets for the City of Manhattan.

By the time he earned his Bachelor of Science degree in mechanical engineering in 1905, he had designed and built his own gasoline tractor. He used this tractor to grade roads, fill silos and thresh grain until 1917.

He received his second degree in 1906 and went to work for the Fairbanks-Morse Company in Beloit, Wisconsin. Emmit's employment was cut short when his father died in 1907 at age sixty-five.

Emmit returned home to work the farm and provide for his family, and an opportunity presented itself after being home for a year. In Cawker City, a blacksmith decided to move to California, and Emmit had the opportunity to buy the blacksmith shop. He moved into a brick building that had been through several owners and had been set up to manufacture automobiles. With a short-term partnership with another K-State graduate, Emmitt set about improving the building. The partnership deteriorated, and the shop name was changed to the E.D. Richardson Cawker Machine and Repair Shop.

Work around the repair shop was dictated by the season, and repair services in a wide variety were offered. Dealerships were added to the lineup and inventory added. Emmit attended the annual Kansas City Gas Engine Show and bought used engines for repair parts and secondhand engines to sell. He was on call to keep the city's engine running in the light plant, and when the engine went down, he installed a temporary engine to keep things running.

Due to Emmit's interest in automobiles, he started repairing them in the building and soon had a dealership for the Maxwell cars; he then took on a Dodge dealership. He also added the Economical Five radio line to the business. All this time, he still had threshing crews working the harvest fields—he had up to four crews working at times. By 1915, he was employing thirty-nine men.

Emmit's mind was always working, constantly thinking on how to make things more efficient, easier and faster. When in the shop, he put those ideas to work. In 1914, he designed and was awarded a patent for improvements in threshing machines. A more profitable venture was his invention of what he called the "Humane Extension Feeder." These were built in lengths from sixteen to forty feet. It took nine years to perfect the design and get the production started. There were many machines added to the factory to make the wooden parts for the feeder.

Three thousand catalogues were printed and distributed in the fall of 1920; in 1921, the first sales representative was hired and put in the field. The feeder was displayed at the Nebraska, Kansas and Oklahoma State Fairs. A Canadian patent was granted in 1922, and sales started to boom. Shipments increased, and a smaller demonstration model was built for display and taken to the Kansas City Implement Dealers Show in 1925.

A poor harvest in 1925 failed to produce the sales that were expected, and another machine appeared—the combine harvester thresher—that hampered sales of parts and machines. Sales slowed, and even though 1930 saw sales of 1,500 Humane Extension Feeders, the Depression slowed all demand for existing products.

This did not stop Emmit's mind from racing ahead, and in 1929, he brought out the Flexible Combine Pick-Up and received a patent on it in 1932. By this time, the Depression had taken hold, and his company had found a niche market in building replacement canvasses for binders, combines and headers. The canvasses he provided were heavier and better made than the originals. This kept older machines working longer when the prices of new machines were just too high. In 1935, when the dust storms arrived, the company produced a sawmill frame that could attach to tractors for cutting cordwood.

In 1939, a new sign was put up that proclaimed E.D. Richardson and Sons Mfg. His oldest son, Paul, who was eighteen, joined the company, as did his second son, Raymond, who was fifteen. Later, sons Danny and Bobby would join the company as well.

With the threat of war, the company decided to build on and expand the factory, and the offer went out that it would buy all steel wheels that anyone had. These were taken apart and straightened, and the rafters for the new addition were made from these recycled wheels. Additions of 50 by 150, 40 by 60 and 48 by 142 square feet were added to the original building. This expanded the facility completely across the block.

The 1941 catalogue offered sixty pages of products, and 111,000 copies were printed and distributed. World War II changed a lot of things. The company was in charge of the community's scrap iron drive, and it succeeded in filling its quota by 150 percent. During this time, a peanut piling machine was designed and built. Many of these went to New Mexico.

The factory was again expanded in 1946 by twelve thousand square feet, and Emmit purchased a comfortable home that had originally been built by Dr. C.L. Brown. He began to have health problems and was confined to bed for two months. On July 24, 1946, Emmit died at age sixty-five.

The passing of Emmit was not the end of Richardson Manufacturing and its association with Cawker City. Emmit's son Raymond took over and enlarged the company with new products, expanding sales all over the country and around the world. His son, Robert who had been in the Marine Corps, also returned and eventually took over management of the company.

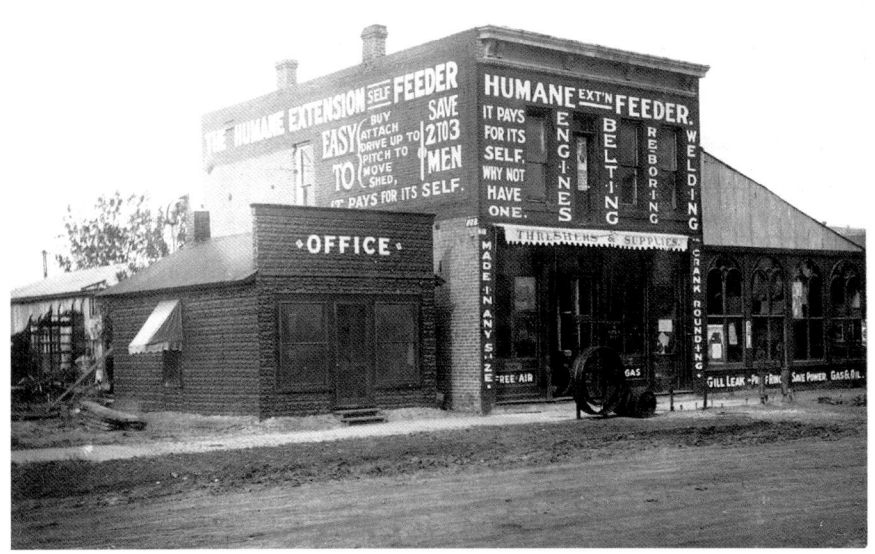

Richardson Manufacturing building, Cawker City, Kansas, circa 1920s. *Courtesy of Cawker City Historical Museum.*

The company made a wide variety of improvements to equipment and the farm attachments that made machines more efficient, one of these being the Stay Kleen straw walker cover. In the 1960s, the AD-Flex Plow was added; this tool could be made up to thirty-five feet wide. After many years of prosperity, the company was sold to Sunflower Manufacturing of Beloit, and all products became part of the Sunflower line. Later, Sunflower was acquired by Agco, which runs the facility today. Robert passed away on January 15, 2008.

Much information and context for Richardson Manufacturing was provided by the Cawker City Historical Museum, whose director is a grandson of the founders.

HINES COMBINE

The wheat farming world was all abuzz in the 1920s when M.J. Hines built and sold his Hines Combine in Hutchinson. The concept of a self-propelled combine thresher was probably being kicked around in a lot of inventors' minds during this period. Hines developed the concept when the predominant way of cutting wheat was with binders and threshing crews who fanned out over the region to get wheat out of the dried bundles and into clean grain ready for milling. The first combines that were operating on the scene in the early 1920s were pull type. It required a tractor or team to operate the machines.

In the push to move from horse farming to power farming, there were several companies that added a PTO (power take off), which ran the machines with a turning shaft from the tractor itself. The first units also could be powered by a separate engine mounted on the combine. The combining of all operations into the machine was a logical progression. The self-propelled combine could save labor, fuel, time and waste. Every time a new field was opened, some wheat was crushed down and lost until the operator was able to keep the tractor in the stubble.

The Marriage Combine, which was developed in the same time frame on the Eagle Canyon Ranch near Mullinville, was the first combine to go on the custom harvest. The five Marriage machines were built in Hutchinson in the old Twin Windmill factory, which may have helped with the design of the Hines or vice versa. It is not known if Marriage knew Mr. Hines, although there is a good chance that they did know each other. Also, Massey-Harris had set up a factory to assemble pull-type combines in Hutchinson, and there are some characteristics that may have been borrowed from both the Hines and the Marriage when that company developed its first self-propelled machines.

There was a downturn in farming after World War I, and there were a lot of companies that did not survive. Hines had his machine in the field in 1920, and the newspapers were busy with articles about it. The hardest thing for Hines was to get the financial backing for his venture. Banks were hesitant, but a Wichita group saw an opportunity and tried to give incentives to the factory to move it to Wichita. Hines preferred to stay in Hutchinson and thought that it was the best location to manufacture and sell his machine.

Another farmer and inventor was K.O. Huff in Protection, Kansas (Comanche County). He had taken the parts of several Ford trucks and Baldwin pull-type combines and created a self-propelled unit. He used the combine to custom-cut in Oklahoma and south-central Kansas. He made no attempt to patent or manufacture his combine.

Reno County was the center of combine development. The Baldwin brothers of Nickerson were also busy designing, building and testing a design that would use a Fordson tractor as a power unit for a self-propelled

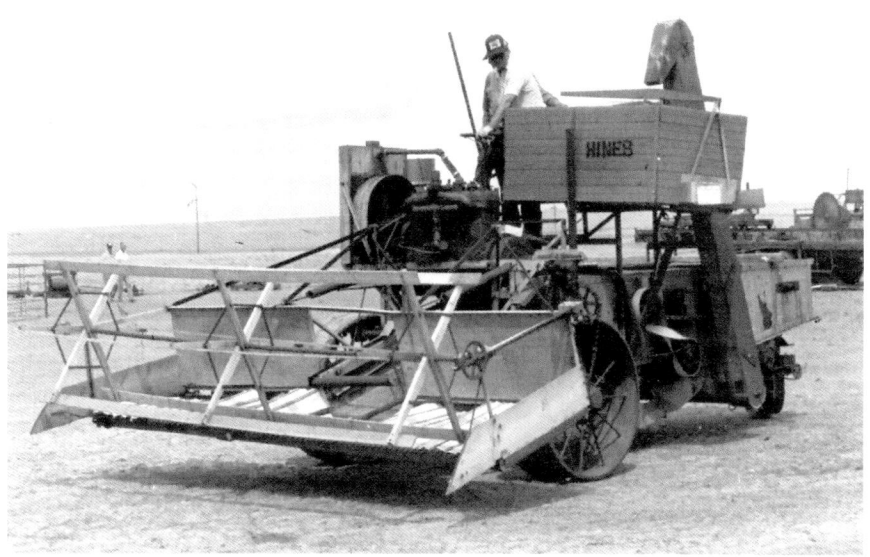

Hines combine. *Courtesy of Robert Taylor.*

combine. This resulted in the Gleaner Baldwin combines, which are still being built in Hesston today.

A total of one hundred Hines combines were produced that could cut at a speed of three miles per hour. The average life of the machines seemed to be about ten years. There are a few operational survivors of the Hines combine still in the hands of collectors today. A great-nephew of Hines, Tony Trenkamp of Spearville, has an original Hines combine and has it restored to operational condition. Several articles have been written on this combine. Tony's wife, Dorothy, and daughter, Vickie Scheve, have a collection of articles, photos and other items about the Hines in a shed on the family farm. They contributed to the history of the machine. There is another known operating Hines Combine that is in the hands of collector Robert Taylor in the Oklahoma panhandle. There is rumor of a third machine that is in pieces, location unknown to this author.

The Hines Combine Company was bought by a group of Wichita investors that had plans to build five thousand machines per year. The Depression scuttled a lot of plans, and this was probably another victim.

JACOB WIENS BULLER: BULLER MANUFACTURING

Jacob Buller's history is akin to the history of the Mennonite immigrants who came to Kansas after emigrating from Ukraine (Molotschna settlement). Jacob was a six-year-old when his family came to the United States, settling first in the rural town of Jansen, Nebraska. Growing up in Nebraska, Jacob showed a talent for mechanical things and eventually invented a snap hitch that went on steam traction engines and, later, on Model Ts and other automobiles.

Jacob was not a successful farmer; when he started manufacturing the coupler, it was a success, but the changing market conditions eventually led to the failure of his company. Jacob also became a partner in a milling business. His father, Peter, ventured into the wheat threshing business, which lead to a business that would sustain Jacob many times in the process of building and rebuilding his companies.

The snap coupler hitch that Jacob invented was not only a time-saving device but also a safety device that eliminated injury to the fingers. The earliest patent filed on the hitch was in 1902. In 1904, he applied for an improved design patent of a lighter and more practical coupler. Orders poured in, but in about 1906, the economy changed—buying extra items on farms was curtailed. This put an end to his budding business.

At about this time, many families were moving away from Jansen, and Jacob decided to move to Kansas, where there were many large settlements of Mennonites. Loading everything on a boxcar, he rented a farm near Aulne, which is in Marion County near Hillsboro. Jacob was not successful as a farmer and soon moved to Hillsboro. There he purchased a butcher shop on Main Street. Being an active man, he soon was also owner of the butcher shop and working in a tin shop across the street. He purchased a one-third interest in a mill and became head engineer. He purchased a home in town and was always looking for another venture to start.

In 1910, with the backing of a family friend, Jacob purchased a threshing machine and a steam traction machine. He put together a crew and went to Osborne County to thresh wheat. The crop in that part of the state was in good shape, and there was a need for threshing crews. After being successful that season, he made a deal to leave his machine with a farmer there and built an addition on a shed to house it over the winter months. The season of threshing was quite an interesting experience and set Jacob on a long-term endeavor of threshing wheat during the season.

Coming home that season restarted Jacob on his inventiveness, and he redesigned the coupler and started up business again. He began advertising in periodicals such as the *American Thresherman* and *Thresherman's Review*. He received many addresses from the ads and started to send price sheets and information to threshermen all over the country. By now, the business building the Buller Coupler was growing so fast that a new building was needed. He was offering catalogues and began to attend state fairs and other exhibitions, selling and taking orders for his hitches. Although the business was growing, it was still not enough to stand on its own, and he continued to subsidize his business with the threshing operation. The next year, the wheat crop was better closer to home, and he shipped the threshing machine and steam tractor back by rail to Hillsboro.

With the successful seasons of 1911 and 1912, Jacob decided to start a second threshing crew, so he went back to the Avery Manufacturing Company factory in Peoria, Illinois, and picked out a new threshing machine and a steam tractor of a new design. Running two outfits at the same time was a challenging business, and to keep up, Jacob ran between the two crews on a motorcycle.

Because of Jacob's activities with the Thresherman's Association, the sales of his Buller Hitches grew. Many people wanted to buy into the company, so it was incorporated. He also was busy designing and patenting new items for the company to manufacture and sell. The company did well until after the war, when there was a depression in the agricultural sector. In 1921, the company failed, and Jacob felt a heavy burden fall on him. Falling back on threshing again, he built himself back up. There was no quit in him, and he started over and began manufacturing products as well as building new products. He eventually paid off all who had lost money on the corporation, as it was not in his faith or character for anyone to lose by investing in him.

Because of his inventiveness and the ability to sell his products, he spent more and more time on the road at fairs and shows. This need gave rise to an invention for which he is probably not given credit: he built a bus. The bus was the forerunner of what we now know as a motor home. In it was storage for products as well as an office, a kitchen and a platform on the back for lounging and speaking. The speaking platform let him pursue his calling as a preacher, and he would preach sermons to crowds. Jacob was an elder in the First Mennonite Church, originally coming from the Alexanderwohl Congregation and later at Goessel.

In total, Jacob built three buses for his travels and business. Whether given credit for it or not, the buses were the first examples of the large motor homes of today. Through his many endeavors, he became a dealer for Case Tractors in Hillsboro and sold Case products for many years.

As equipment changed over the years, there were other inventions that soon became the main products for the Buller Manufacturing Company. One of these was a stationary and mounted saw that would be used to cut firewood. Even today, many of the Buller saws can be found still operating.

In the late 1930s, Jacob was able to get a contract selling his product through the *Montgomery Ward Catalogue*. This pushed the company to be the largest employer in Hillsboro other than the school district. His last patent was in 1935, for the design of sawblade setting tools. As Jacob grew older, he turned over more and more control to his sons, and they carried on the company for many years.

Buller Manufacturing invented LP gas conversion kits for tractors and equipment in the 1950s. One day, a manufacturer happened to be in town on his way to find a company to build a full-vision tractor cab in Kansas City. Eating at the local café, the businessman, Mr. Stucky, was directed to Buller across the street. Staying until the next day, he made an agreement for the cab to be built by Buller. Over time, the company supplied five thousand tractor cabs. The company also did work for the Hesston Corporation.

Some of the heavy machines in the factory were designed and built by Jacob and were used until the day the company was shut down. The final son, Levi, retired and sold the company in 1974. Jacob's grandson was called by the new owner, who wanted to know if he wanted all the wooden patterns that his grandfather had made. Every pattern over the years was carved by hand by Jacob and kept in storage for the possibility that the patterns would be needed again in the future.

Virgil Litke, Jacob's grandson, came down, and all the patterns were brought out of storage and put in his truck. Virgil has the collection, as well as many other items from over the years. During a celebration in Hillsboro, the artifacts were put on display on Main Street in Hillsboro.

Virgil Litke authored a book detailing the life of his grandfather and the many experiences that he and his family had over the years. Jacob Buller was born in 1869 and died in 1946. The obituary from the *Mennonite Weekly Review* noted, "One of the largest funerals in recent months was that of Jacob W. Buller, enterprising businessman of this city, held at First Mennonite Church on Friday afternoon, March 15. Mr. Buller died March 12, at the age of 77 years. Unusually gifted in mechanical lines, Mr. Buller was a widely known manufacturer and inventor. Few if any engaged in such a wide range of activities, which included farming, threshing rig operator, manufacturing of

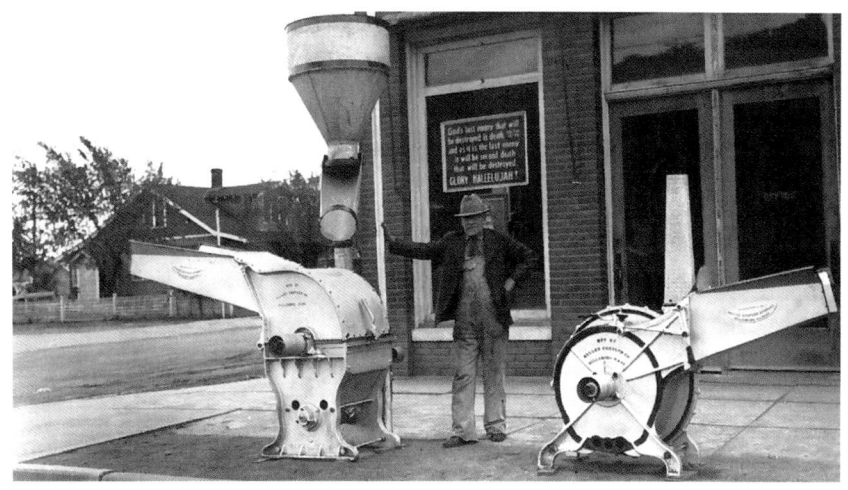

Jacob Buller with machines in front of a factory, circa 1930s. *Courtesy of Virgil Litke.*

saw frames for Montgomery Ward, butcher shop owner, and inventor of tools and farm equipment."

The book that Mr. Litke wrote contributed a lot of the information for this story. It can still be purchased online: *A Journey with My Grandfather, Jacob W. Buller*. It was published in 1986 and is a good read.

THRESHING STONES

Being a native of the Wheat State, the various ways of historically threshing out the grain from the straw and chaff is something that is just absorbed over the years from being from a farm family and running combines for family and others. Although the author's heritage comes mostly through Germany, our family was not a part of the German groups (primarily Mennonite but also Volga Catholics) that came through the Ukraine, a part of Russia.

The threshing stone was generally cut from limestone, with several large notches carved into the circular stone of approximately twenty-three to twenty-four inches in diameter. Many Kansas-made stones were up to thirty inches in diameter. The stones were used on a threshing floor made of clay that was smoothed and baked in the heat of the summer sun. The stone was pulled by one horse that was ridden in a circle over the stalks of wheat two or three times. This process separated the seed from the straw and chaff.

In the Ukraine, it is not uncommon to see stones in front of homes or other buildings. Many see the stones and never give them a thought or just don't realize what the stones are and what they represent. Glenn Ediger, whose background is Mennonite, began a journey to find and document the remaining threshing stones in Kansas. The obvious ones—like in front of Bethel College, at the Kaufman Museum and at Buhler High School—were readily apparent. Ediger spent years talking to old-timers, going to cafés, visiting museums and just driving through the five counties that are heavily Mennonite in population.

In his book, *Leave No Threshing Stone Unturned*, Ediger described his journey in the quest to find and document all of the remaining threshing stones in Kansas. It was research that took years to complete, and there is still a stone or two out there that may be displaced or just forgotten. As of publication of this book, the number stands at one hundred: twenty-nine on public display and seventy-one on private property.

In his research, he found stones that were not originally threshing stones. He also found a few that were turned on their sides and used as salt licks. He found no evidence of any in the Swiss Volhynian Mennonite communities, like in the Pretty Prairie area. He found little evidence of Volga German usage. Although there were rumors of stones used in the Ellis County area, and stones found appear to have come from the same quarries and stonemasons as others, there was no direct evidence of usage.

Of the known stones in North America, ninety-one are in Kansas and one each in Nebraska, Colorado, Missouri, Indiana, North Dakota and Texas. Three are known to be in Canada, and there are twenty known replicas.

Threshing stones were not used long in this country because of the design of the threshing machines that were in existence before the migration of the Mennonites to this country. Turkey Red wheat was introduced to this country by the Mennonites. Its varieties thrive on the climate and soil of the Great Plains and led to the wheat industry as we know it today.

What is more interesting than just the search for the threshing stones is the story of the hardships that Germans went through by migrating to the Ukraine under the sponsorship of Catherine the Great, as well as the subsequent hardships they suffered in leaving there and immigrating to the United States and starting with very little on the plains.

Copies of the book *Leave No Threshing Stone Unturned* are available at the museum in Inman. It is worth your time to spend a day there—call ahead for an appointment to ensure that that someone is available to open and take you on a tour.

MAX BLUE: BLUE STAR BOATS

In the sport of motorboat racing, up until Max Blue introduced Blue Star Boats, all racers were called "runabouts." They were very light with an outboard motor and went really fast. Before Max Blue, all boats were wooden or fiberglass. It was the thinking of the time that a metal boat could not be a successful competitor in the sport, but Max changed all that.

Max Blue worked in the aircraft industry in Wichita and lived with his family in Goddard, the first town west of Wichita on Highway 54. Max worked with sheet aluminum and started building boats in his garage in Goddard as a hobby. The hobby turned into a business. Max used to take his family to the boat races near Manhattan, and there he met a farmer from Harper County named John Jordan. As they visited one day at the Lake Afton races, Max was told by Jordan that he could build a successful racing hull if he incorporated the features that John wanted in a boat. Max built the boat, and the results were spectacular.

John Jordan eventually set a new speed record in Class B. His wife, Patricia, won Class A events since she was light enough to race in that class (John was too heavy). They won many races from Minnesota to Texas, and the name Blue Star Boats started to become famous. Eventually, Max would

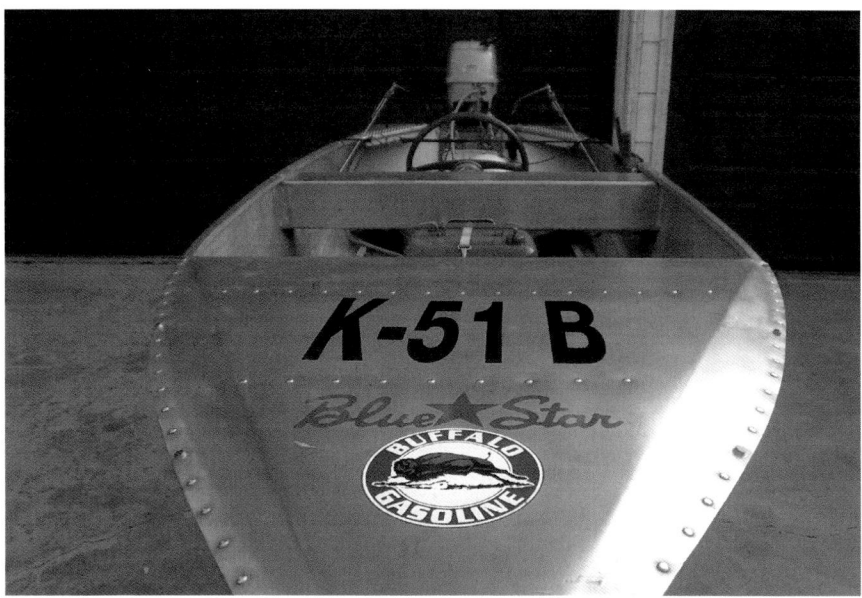

Blue Star racing boat. *Courtesy of Ronald Lietha.*

rent a building on Main Street in Goddard and began manufacturing. At one time, he employed twenty-eight people.

As a youngster, the author went to Goddard Schools, the building that would house Churchman's Honey in the back part. Over the years, several businesses would rent the building on Main Street. In 1953, Max moved Blue Star Boats out of Kansas and to Miami, Oklahoma. They were building about one thousand boats per year at that time.

Blue Star built boats in a ten-foot sixty-pound hull, a twelve-foot, and fourteen-foot standard open hull, a twelve-foot deluxe, and high-speed runabouts of eleven and a half and thirteen and a half feet. The boats have a lot of collector interest today; Ronald Lietha from north-central Wisconsin is a collector who has a boat like the one John Jordan used to set the records. It has been restored to be a perfect replica of the original. Mr. Lietha helped with information and photos for this story.

GODDARD SNAKE PIT

There are many things that happened in Kansas that are not well known, and this makes documentation very difficult. The story of the Goddard Snake Pit is one that the author has to take strictly by eyewitness testimony. Try as hard as I could, there was just nothing to document what happened. But the story needs to be recorded.

Goddard was built as result of the railroad moving the planned westward track one and a half miles south of where it was supposed to go. As the railroad was about to be built, the town of Blendon was being built at the Ten Mile corner. The Ten Mile corner is now 167th West and Maple Street. This was the original route of the Kingman Trail and then the Old Cannonball, which was the original US Highway 54. Cannonball was named after Cannonball Green, who ran a stage line west of Wichita and other places before the railroads were built.

In 1883, construction began on the railroad, and the depot at Goddard, which was started as a railcar, was under construction for an 1884 completion date. As with many of the railroad stops, since the trains were steam-driven, a hand-dug well was required. Steam locomotives could only go so far before taking on water. Also, there needed to be locations periodically along the tracks for towns to build and be able to service customers. Selling the land granted to the railroads and the revenues from the farmers made the extension of the railroads possible.

With the conversion to diesel electric locomotives, there was no longer any need for the wells. In some locations, the wells became a part of the municipal water systems—or, like in Greensburg, tourist attractions. In Goddard, the railroad chose to just fill in the well. Everything that could be found was dumped into the old well to close it up. Old cars, rocks, old bundles of wire, steel and dirt—all was put into the hole just adjacent to the depot and then forgotten.

Dale Hosey was the depot master in the 1950s and lived just north of the depot. Sometimes his kids would come over and visit him while he was working or run messages to him. That is why what happened is a bit nerve-rattling, especially for Dale's wife. The story she told this author was one I had never heard before. (The author is a third-generation graduate of Goddard High School, and the inspiration for my interest in history was Dale Churchman, who was a history teacher and local businessman. This is a story even Mr. Churchman had never heard.)

In the research for this book on another story about Max Blue and Blue Star Boats, a former classmate contacted me and said that Virginia Hosey wondered why I wasn't doing a story on the Snake Pit. I was intrigued and contacted her for an interview. This is the story she told.

One day in the 1950s—around 1953 or before—Dale Hosey came home and called for help from several men in town to grab their shotguns and shells and come to the depot. It seemed the old well had collapsed and was open again. This was chilling for Virginia because one of the boys had just walked over the spot an hour before it fell in. Instead of revealing all the things put down the well to fill it, everything was gone—apparently pulled away by the underground river. The bottom of the hole was full of snakes. It is not known what kind of snakes. Dale is no longer with us, and there was apparently no record of the event made with any details.

Dale Hosey was able to get Wilber Floyd and Max Blue to come down, and they shot the snakes until nothing moved in the pit. The railroad contracted for the well to be properly refilled. The area has never shown any settling since, so the old well site and snake pit are now only memories—though not memories for very many.

Since the author grew up in the community and I am personally acquainted with most of the parties involved, I put my faith in the story that the snake pit is true. It is a wonder to me that very few ever knew about the incident ever happening, and it would have been lost completely if Virginia had not talked to me personally.

CERO'S CANDY

In the *Wichita Beacon* newspaper on December 20, 1897, the following ad was placed:

> *CHRISTMAS CANDIES*
> *PETER CERO'S, 896 E. DOUGLAS AVE.*
> *Bon-Bons, Cream Candies, Mixed Candies. Home Made Cream candies,*
> *9 cents a pound, 3 pounds for 25 cents*
> *Cream Nuggets, 13 cents, 2 pounds for 25 cents*
> *Home Made Coconut Candy. A large assortment of all kinds of candies.*
> *New crop of nuts 2 pounds for 25 cents*
> *Give us a call and you will be a satisfied customer. We have 2½ tons of candy on hand.*

Peter Cero was a Greek sailor who jumped ship at New Orleans in order to immigrate to the United States. He went to work for the railroads as a laborer and was working on the railroad in Wichita when he began to have bad health. Left behind by his crew, he had to make a living. He started to make pies and other sweet treats, and in 1885 he purchased a building at 900 East Douglas in Wichita.

The business grew and grew, and in 1902, he brought his nephew, Edward, to town from Poros, Greece, to help in his business. Edward soon took over daily operations and added ice cream to the menu in 1905. Edward sent for his wife, Ethel, in 1907 to join him in the business. They soon had a son, John, who grew up in the business. The candy shop prospered, and in 1927, they moved to a new location at 1227 East Douglas. The business prospered through the 1930s and 1940s. Ed retired in 1950, and his son, John E., took over the business.

When Highway 54 was built through town, called Kellogg, a new building was constructed, and Cero's moved to 2919 East Kellogg. There the company prospered for many years. John died suddenly in 1974, leaving his wife, Ethel, and sons, Ed and Dean, running the business alone. The family continued to innovate and grow and negotiated the pitfalls of being a small business. Government regulations and then the decision to rebuild and expand Kellogg into a limited-access interstate-quality road left the building isolated—it could be seen, but it was difficult to drive to.

The business faced many challenges over the years. During World War II, there was rationing and shortages of sugar and chocolate. Then the

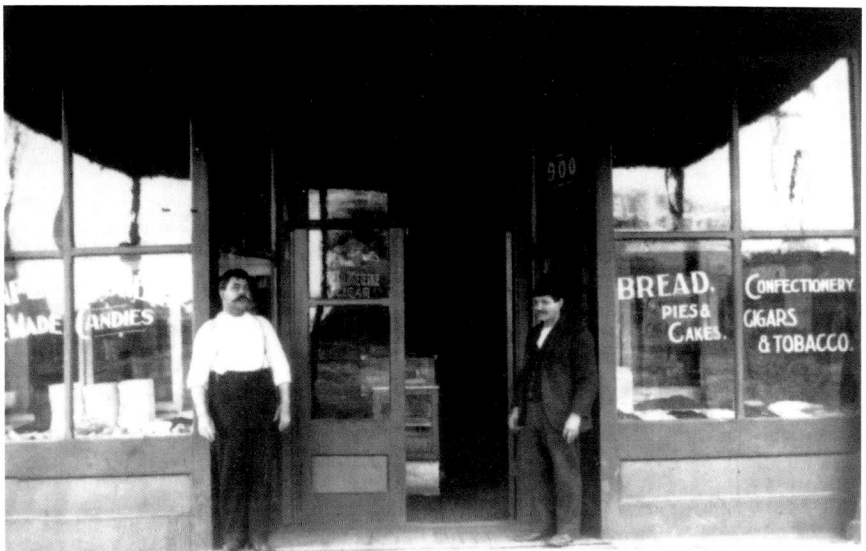

Cero's Candy Shop, circa 1890s. *Courtesy of Wichita-Sedgwick County Historical Museum.*

piling-on of regulations from local, state and federal governments caused John to tell an OSHA inspector that "this is not General Mills you know!" In the 1960s, everything bad was blamed on chocolate. The isolation of the business from the highway was devastating. The shop had loyal customers and long-term employees who kept them going and facing each challenge. Being isolated from the highway allowed them to sue, and they won a judgment in their favor—though the city never paid. The building was finally sold in 2009.

Prospective buyers for the company continued to make offers to the family, and the business was sold to the Mental Health Association of South Central Kansas. The association ran the store as a job training and nurturing environment for adults with special needs. After the business was bought in 2009, the workshop was run for a while, but it soon became too much for them to handle. In 2011, the company returned to private ownership when mother and daughter Pam and Darcy Bishop purchased it. The Bishops were longtime customers of Cero's, so it was natural for them to buy and operate it. The business was back on East Douglas again, just two blocks from where it all started. However, due to health issues, the Bishops were forced to sell the company. Again, the spirit of the entrepreneur stepped up, and the business was bought by the Albrecht family. They had been looking for a business for a year.

The Cero family owned and operated the candy business for 117 years in Wichita. Although the names have changed, the traditions of quality and customer service remain in Wichita.

DR. SAMUEL J. CRUMBINE

Dr. Sam Crumbine was Kansas secretary of health in 1906 and a leading medical reformer. He led several statewide campaigns against disease and was instrumental in the development of a device often used yet totally taken for granted: the fly swatter. In fact, he is responsible for the name. Watching a baseball game, an excited fan shouted, "Did you see him swat that fly?" when the batter hit a fly ball over the fence. Dr. Sam believed that many diseases were spread by flies, and the campaign slogan was born.

Enter Frank Rose of Weir City and his Boy Scouts. The scout troop was building wire screens to put on windows in town to help keep out flies. The leftover pieces were cut into squares and nailed to yardsticks. They called them fly bats. Rose showed them to Dr. Sam, and he called them "fly swatters," and they became a new health tool.

Fly swatters were soon being handed out at the Kansas State Fair, county fairs and local anti-fly parades all over the state. Its popularity soon spread all over, and although there are many who claim that the fly swatter was invented elsewhere, it happened in Kansas first.

Flies were not the only health problem that Dr. Sam fought against. Tuberculosis was a deadly and common problem in the nineteenth and twentieth centuries. The common method of having a drink at public wells at the time was a tin cup that hung for everyone to use. Dr. Sam wanted to put an end to this practice and invented the paper cup. He convinced the manufacturers of the Dixie Cup to print his slogan from another campaign, "Don't Spit on Sidewalk," on the disposable cups. But Dr. Sam went a step further. He approached brick makers in southeast Kansas to create bricks with the slogan on them, and they were sent all over the country to combat TB. They are very collectable today.

The use of disposable cups, paper towels and many other common disease-prevention practices goes back to the fervor of Dr. Sam. If you are a fan of 1950s and 1960s television, the persona of Dr. Sam should be familiar. Dr. Sam had a practice in Dodge City. He authored a book called *Autobiography of a Pioneer on the Frontier of Public Health*. In this book, he described his years of practice on

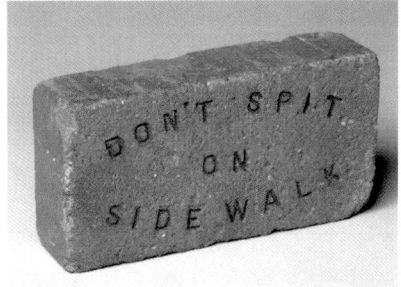

Above: Anti-TB brick. Dr. Crumbine had Kansas brick makers create these, which were sent all over the country. *Courtesy of Kansas State Historical Society.*

Right: Dr. Samuel Crumbine. *Courtesy of Kansas State Historical Society.*

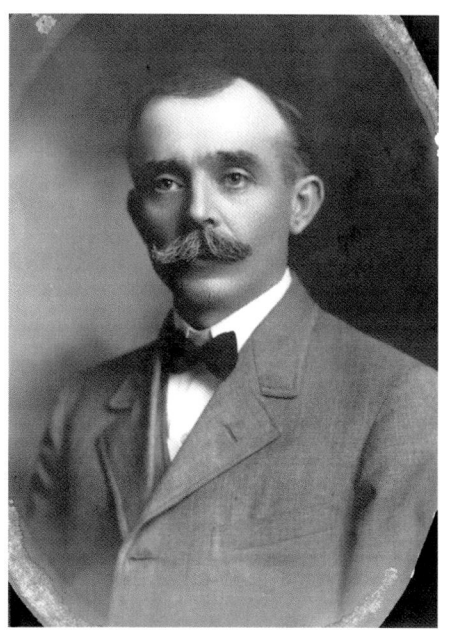

the frontier in Dodge City. He was in Dodge City starting in 1890 and was the model and inspiration of the character of "Doc Adams" on TV's *Gunsmoke*, a part played so well by Kansan Milburn Stone.

During his tenure on the State Board of Health, Dr. Sam was appointed to the University of Kansas Medical School. He left Kansas in 1923 and served as executive director of the American Child Health Association. He retired to Long Island, New York, although he returned often to Kansas for speaking engagements. He died on July 12, 1954. The Crumbine Award was established in 1955 in his memory and is awarded each year by the food and drug industry to encourage public health.

J.A. HOCKETT: HOCKETT STERLING TRACTOR

In 1896, J.A. Hockett was a broom corn commission dealer in Sterling. In 1893, Hockett and three others started a company called the Gasoline Thresher and Plow Company in Sterling. Hockett invented and received a patent for a gasoline traction engine in 1896. Even though the company was headquartered in Sterling and the traction engine was named the Sterling, it

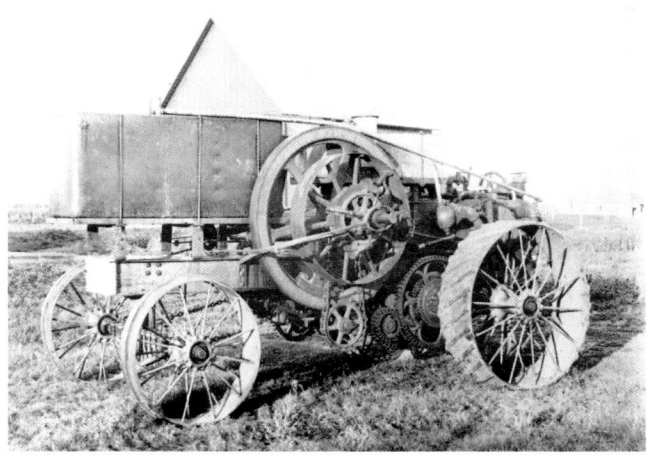

Hockett Tractor. *Courtesy of the Wisconsin Historical Society.*

was apparently built in Kansas City. There is a lot of confusion today over the Hockett tractor because of another traction engine built in Canada that was also named the Sterling.

The numbering of the engine suggests that it was powered by an Erd engine, which was very common for the time and the next twenty years, powering traction engines of many makes. What makes the tractor special is the fact that it was the first light gasoline traction engine offered for sale commercially.

Surviving models of the Hockett or Sterling are not known to exist. The traction engine was advertised in many newspapers of the time. Even so, it is very difficult to find any information on the engine. There is one magazine of the day that suggests that the traction engine was actually built in St. Louis. It is believed that several prototypes were built, and the fact that the company lasted three years suggests that there was actually production of the tractor.

In the earliest comparison lists, the Hockett is noted among the earliest models being offered. The American Society of Mechanical Engineers Bulletin from Charles City lists the chartering of companies as 1889 Charter, 1892 Froelich, 1892 Patterson, 1895 Hockett/Sterling, 1894 Van Duzen, 1899 Morton, 1901 Kinnard Hanes and 1901 Hart Parr.

The incorporation of the Gasoline Thresher and Plow Company of Sterling and Kansas City, Kansas, had a capital stock of $100,000. Directors and officers were P. Hockett, R.A. Steward, P.P. Truehart, W.W. Webb and J.A. Hockett.

In *Robertson's Book of Firsts*, the Hockett/Sterling traction engine was the first to be advertised for sale; the Hart Parr is considered to be the first successful gasoline tractor to be sold in the United States. At this time, the large steam traction engines were used for sod breaking and powering threshing machines. The concept of a lightweight tractor was not something that would catch on for a while, and the small and less expensive traction engines like the Hockett or Hart Parr would soon replace the horse and the use of horse-drawn equipment of the time. Historical texts suggest that several Hockett tractors were used in the Sterling and Lyons area for several years.

The Hockett/Sterling traction engine may have been another idea that was too far ahead of its time to be successful. It would be the same problem with the automobile and airplane.

BARNETT HASSOCKS

Cawker City is not just known for its huge ball of twine (the largest in the world). The town is also famous for hassocks. George and son E.J. Barnett made and sold them all over the nation. Although plastic is something that has the reputation of being cheap and not very desirable, at one time plastic was a new and wondrous material. After World War II and the baby boom, plastic was the latest whiz-bang product that captured everyone's attention.

George Barnett built the first "Stow Away" hassock, starting while living on a farm in Nebraska. After moving to Cawker City, his son managed a store and decided that the product was popular enough to build and sell. The immediate success of the product prompted going into business, building a factory and starting production of the hassocks in a big way. The business boomed, and soon Barnett and son were building hassocks day and night. They started to hire others to help with production and shipping.

So, what is a hassock? It was a foot rest that had a hollow space to store things such as clothing. The hassocks were made of plastic, and soon the company started to add other upholstered pieces of furniture to the line. One such item was a plastic "cedar" bench. The bench was made of plastic, but there was some kind of embedded substance such that, when opened, the storage compartment smelled like a cedar chest and the clothing stored inside would be protected from moths and other insects, just like clothing in a real cedar chest would be.

Cawker City in the 1940s and 1950s was a town of only one thousand residents. There was one other manufacturer in town that was a major employer: the Richardson Company, which made farm equipment. When the Barnett Company built a new factory, the result was a lot of activity in the town. And as sales grew, so did the factory, with several additions being made to the building, according to the local newspaper. The business boomed so much that the railroad depot had to add another agent in order to handle

Kansas Oddities

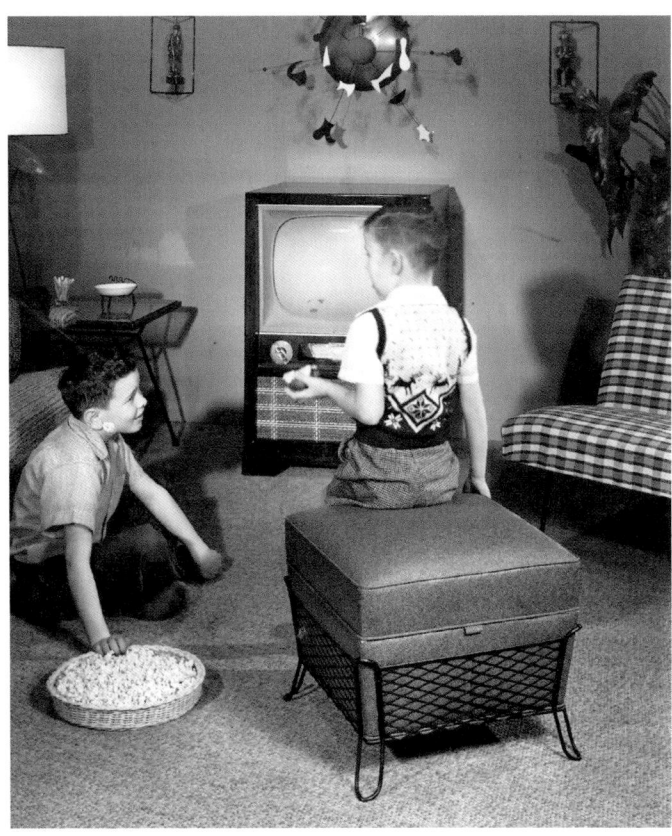

Barnett Hassock advertisement. *Courtesy of Cawker City Historical Museum.*

all the shipping of the Barnetts' products. Eventually, George turned over operations to his son and only helped out with some design work now and then. This would have been around 1953.

An article from the May 28, 1953 issue of the *Cawker City Ledger* noted the latest news: "This week approximately 15 million subscribers of the *Saturday Evening Post* and *Living for Young Homemakers* will see pictures of a product being manufactured in our bustling little city of Cawker." This was part of a national advertising program pushing Barnett's upholstered storage hassocks, vacuum cleaner chests, Hollywood bed ends and other products. The company had designed a hassock that housed both the General Electric and Eureka canister-type cleaners. GE and Eureka dealers placed many large orders for this product. At the time, the company had five thousand dealers nationwide and produced a catalogue that was distributed nationwide. The company also had fifty salesmen who worked direct sales. The company provided a lot of work for the local newspaper publisher, which printed the company's catalogues.

After George retired from the company, it only took a year for him to get bored. So, with one of his original employees, he rented a small building and started to build some items that he had designed. He just could not stand to do nothing and made a few things to sell. In 1964, George's son, E.J. (Edward John), decided to retire and sold the company to Leo Bruggeman and Lawrence Lutz. The Burnett factory shut down, and the new owners restarted the business with the help of former owner E.J. The factory slowly built up its employee numbers and branched out into new products, for a time manufacturing mattresses for a camper manufacturer. E.J. also owned the Big B Restaurant from 1952 until 1964. He then moved to Stockton and established a country club.

E.J. Barnett stayed on with the new owners. Sales had slowed, and when one of the two camper manufacturers went bankrupt, the company eventually closed.

Information on the story of the company was provided in large part by the Cawker City Historical Museum—a big thanks for its work and assistance.

McPHERSON WETLANDS

The "Great American Desert" is what early explorers called the central part of the United States. Finding an unending expanse of grassland and no forest was, at the very least, intimidating to the people moving through to the western side of the continent. Little did they realize what lay ahead on the vast expanse of grass. There were huge wetlands that were stopover sites and homes to hundreds of animal species and a treasure-trove of food for the native tribes as they traveled the area.

The most well-known wetlands are Cheyenne Bottoms and Quivira. Cheyenne Bottoms is a freshwater wetland now controlled by Kansas Wildlife, Parks and Tourism. Quivira is a salt marsh, a National Wildlife Refuge under the control of the U.S. Fish and Wildlife Service. Each is a major stopover for migratory birds from ducks and geese to whooping cranes. But there was a third major wetland on the plains: the McPherson Wetlands.

The McPherson Wetlands covered an area from just south of Conway, down past McPherson and Inman, reaching down the Little Arkansas River to near Valley Center. The estimated coverage of the McPherson Valley Wetland was about thirty thousand acres. Water levels fluctuated with the amount of rainfall, so the water-covered areas would vary from year to year.

In the 1800s, the area was an economic boon to the local towns of Conway and McPherson. Hunters from Chicago, Kansas City, St. Louis and all points back east would arrive by train to shoot massive numbers of birds. Local residents would guide most of these hunters, and it was a sizeable business for the area. The locals would also market hunt. Barrel loads and wagon loads of birds were shot and put on the trains that took them back east for the meat markets.

One man described a hunt that was so successful that he was sent back to town to find a double-sided wagon to haul all the birds into town. He estimated that it took about two thousand birds to fill the wagon, and when it came to town, everyone was able to take birds home for their own use off the wagon. Another guide said that he would allow hunting until noon and then stop. That gave everyone enough time to pick up all the birds they had shot to take back to town. It was said that even with the huge numbers of birds shot each year, there were ample birds to return and nest.

A major portion of the wetlands was in McPherson County. The migration of Mennonite settlers and farmers into the region would soon start changing the function and look of the land. Large numbers of Mennonite settlers were transported by the Santa Fe Railroad, and many settled in Marion, McPherson, Harvey and Reno Counties. The settlers were very astute farmers and had been allowed by Catherine the Great to follow their faith and conscience in the Ukraine. The area of the Ukraine they came from is similar to Kansas in temperament and geology. As the change in rulers happened, the nonviolent beliefs of the people were challenged when it came to expected military service. It soon became apparent that migrating was the only hope of being allowed to stay true to their beliefs.

The Mennonites were a very thrifty and innovative agricultural people. As the land was being settled, there were the beginnings of trying to farm the wetland areas. Draining became a subject of conversation. Some of the areas were as small as one acre, with many others ranging into five and ten acres. The largest was the Big Basin, which covered several thousand acres, and that became the subject for draining and farming.

The wetlands area was originally the course of the Smoky Hill River. The river used to drain south and join the Arkansas River. Over time, the river changed course and flowed east, eventually joining the Missouri River. The resulting lowlands were a chain of shallow areas with two large lakes that averaged around five feet deep. Lake Inman is thought to be the only naturally occurring lake and the largest natural lake in Kansas. Starting around the turn of the twentieth century, the size of the wetlands has dropped 90 percent from its original extent.

OGDEN PUBLICATIONS: *MOTHER EARTH NEWS*

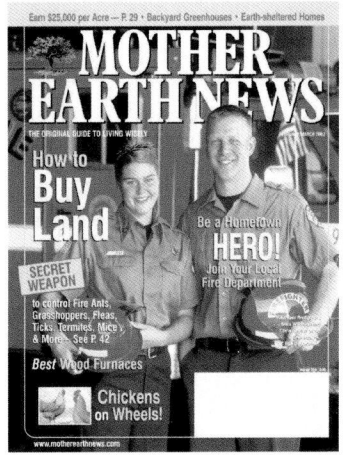

Mother Earth News. Courtesy of Ogden Publications.

Mother Earth News is a magazine that was started in the 1970s by John and Jane Shuttleworth in Madison, Ohio. The magazine was started on a budget of $1,500 and an idea. The subject of the magazine was the back-to-the-land movement that was starting to grow out of the 1960s. It combined the interests of the ecological movement and the idea of self-sufficiency. The magazine concentrated on do-it-yourself and how-to articles.

There were articles on homebuilding, farming, gardening and entrepreneurism. There was a wide range of subjects such as geodesic domes, hunting and food storage, as well as a regular column on amateur radio. Alternative energy was a frequent subject, going into practical solar, wind and ethanol. Another popular feature was the "Plowboy Interview," which featured environmental leaders and others.

The magazine gathered a large following of back-to-the-landers, hippies, survivalists, suburban dwellers, city dwellers wanting to move to the country and rural people who found the articles useful. John Shuttleworth is quoted in a "Plowboy Interview" in 1975 noting that "in short, I think we live in an unbelievably marvelous Garden of Eden. We are surrounded by miraculous life forms, almost without number, kept alive by a mysterious, interwoven, self-replenishing support system that, with all our scientific breakthroughs, we still do not understand. And yet, as favored as we are by all this real wealth, we somehow perversely prefer to spend almost all our waking hours interpreting the sum total of the reality in terms of a narrow and distorted, strictly human-centered concept of money."

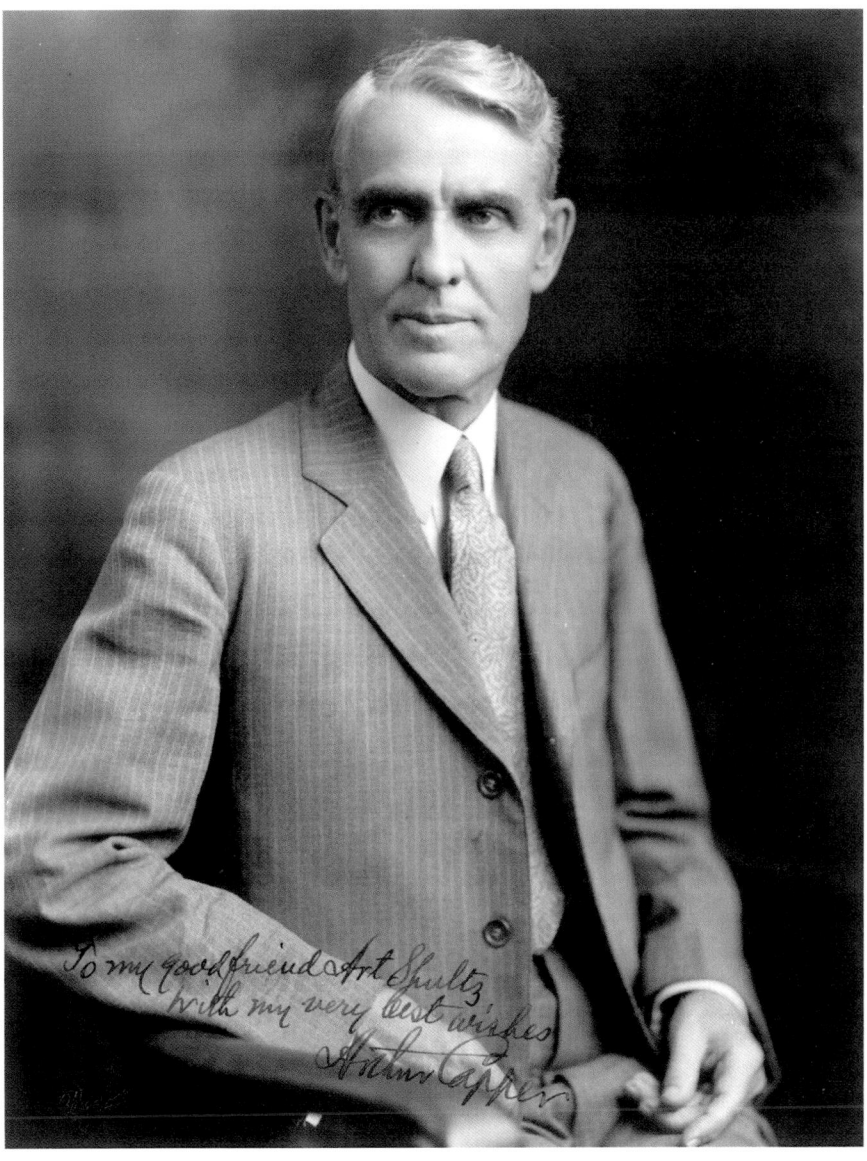

Arthur Capper. *Courtesy of Kansas State Historical Society.*

The magazine had opened the Eco-Village, a six-hundred-acre research facility in North Carolina. In 1979, editor Bruce Woods and two other employees bought the magazine. The Eco-Village was a large research center that utilized hands-on approaches to the articles and subjects of the magazine and the concepts subscribed to the magazine and its mission.

Twenty thousand people per year would take seminars at the site. A radio program was aired nationwide that brought more attention to the magazine and its mission.

The back-to-the-land movement started to slow down in the 1980s, and readership started to lag. The company was sold to the New American Company, which redesigned the magazine and repositioned it as the "Original Country Magazine." A number of employees left the magazine and started *Back Home Magazine*. New American stopped publishing its magazines and sold to Sussex Publishers in New York City. It owned the magazine until it was purchased by Ogden Publishers and moved to offices in Topeka, Kansas.

How it came to be produced in Kansas goes back to Arthur Capper and *Grit Magazine*. Capper was a colorful publisher and politician and a story all his own in Kansas. When his empire was sold, it was purchased by another journalism legend in Kansas, Oscar Stanley Stauffer. Both Capper and Stauffer played important roles in Kansas and the history of journalism in Kansas.

When the Stauffer empire was sold, the Ogden Publications Group—which started with similar humble roots—became a multimillion-dollar business. Ogden had purchased the *Grit* periodicals and Capper Insurance, which had an office in Topeka. When the company purchased *Mother Earth News*, its staff was moved to Topeka and now is part of a Kansas institution.

FRANK FERGUSON: AUTOMOBILE THRESHER

If you are from the Bellville area, the Ferguson name is very familiar. The Ferguson family has been involved in the fire department for generations. Part of that heritage comes from Frank Ferguson. It would be easy to confuse the name with the popular farm equipment company, but there is no connection other than ideas for improving the process of farming. In the process of inventing a new concept in threshing wheat, Frank Ferguson had to invent a component that was necessary for all trucks, tractors and automobiles to be practical successes: the clutch.

Frank Ferguson was a blacksmith and machinist and is remembered as a man who could build anything. At the time, the threshing of crops was done by large machines that were pulled to the fields, and the shocks, or bundles, of cut crops were brought to the machine to be fed into the thresher. The thresher would separate the grain from the chaff and straw, depositing the grain on one side for sacking or hauling and blowing the straw on a stack that was used for livestock bedding. In the early days, the power units were steam traction engines, and some of the straw would be twisted and used to burn in the machine. Later on, as the tractor was developed, tractors replaced the steam engine. The threshing machine was powered by a belt drive.

In an idea that would simplify the process, Frank developed a unit that was self-propelled and incorporated this unit into the thresher design. This was the forerunner of the self-propelled combine. The unique thing about the power unit was that it was designed to be separated from the threshing unit and could be used as a farm tractor or as a vehicle that could be driven to town. The innovation at the heart of the unit was the clutch. It solved the problem of engaging and disengaging the engine from the transmission. This invention would be the item that would eventually ruin the future of the new company that was formed around the automobile thresher.

After building a prototype and working it in the area, there was a great sense of hope about the practicality of the machine and the future of the company. The local paper proclaimed that Frank would be the next millionaire and was confident that the prosperity of the company would translate into prosperity for the community. The community turned out as the new automobile thresher was loaded onto a railcar for a trip to Kansas City for the National Farm Equipment Show. While there, the thresher was the hit of the show, and offers from many major companies to buy all available company stock and offers for outright purchase were tendered. Several thousand dollars was taken in orders for the machine. The future for Ferguson and the company looked bright.

Ten machines were built and put into the fields, but there were problems on the horizon. The innovativeness of the automobile thresher inspired many other companies and inventors. Within two years, a company was organized in Minnesota that created its own version of the automobile thresher. Many of the machinists and companies were stealing the technology, even though it was patented. To protect an item from patent infringement, unfortunately, requires lawyers and lawsuits to pursue the actions.

One major company appropriated the clutch technology, and this caused Frank and his company to take legal action. Frank could only afford one lawyer, but his opponent had the ability to spend millions in the lawsuit. This was mentioned in many sources, and the major company was never named. When interviewing Frank's granddaughter, Phyllis Ferguson, she gave me the name of the company that stole the technology: the Ford Motor Company. Soon, many tractor companies were developing the clutch and other variations of Frank's technology. For all practical purposes, the invention of the clutch made power farming and locomotion possible.

The original prototype was powered by a Moline boat engine. The ability for later models to be separated from the threshing unit would be adopted by a few farm manufacturers in later years. The invention of the unit tractor can find a direct link to Frank's original idea. Ten units were built and served for many years. They were acclaimed as very reliable machines. The last known unit was in Canada in the 1950s. The original machine ended up being cut up, and there are no known units left.

COLBY PLOW BOY TRACTOR: JONES MANUFACTURING

In the *Standard Catalog of Farm Tractors, 1890–1980*, there is a short listing with a picture of a tractor that would, it was hoped, make Colby a major farm equipment manufacturing center. But something went wrong. The short article reports that the company was founded in 1910 and built tractors, and then there was no further mention of the company after that. The periodical listed that no information was available as to the specifications of the Plow Boy. If you put the words "Plow Boy" into a search engine, more than likely you will come up with a picture of a Plowboy and Plowman Tractor, built in Iowa.

The story of the Plow Boy is another Kansas saga involving a need and a dreamer or group of dreamers that decided they could fill the need themselves while also hoping to create an industry and get rich in the process. But here is the rest of the story, as much as can be found by the Prairie Museum of Art and History.

The only record found by the museum is an article from the pages of the *Prairie Drummer* newspaper in Colby, dated February 20, 1965. The story starts with three large farmers from the Thomas County area: I.W. Haynes, Billy Walker and Jim Fike. The three of them were farming on a large scale in Thomas County. Steam power was transitioning to gas and distillate power. Irwin Willis Haynes was a farmer, seed and grain dealer, thresherman and inventor. In the fall of 1910, he invented the tractor called the Colby Plow Boy. There was a foundry east of the courthouse in Colby called the Jones

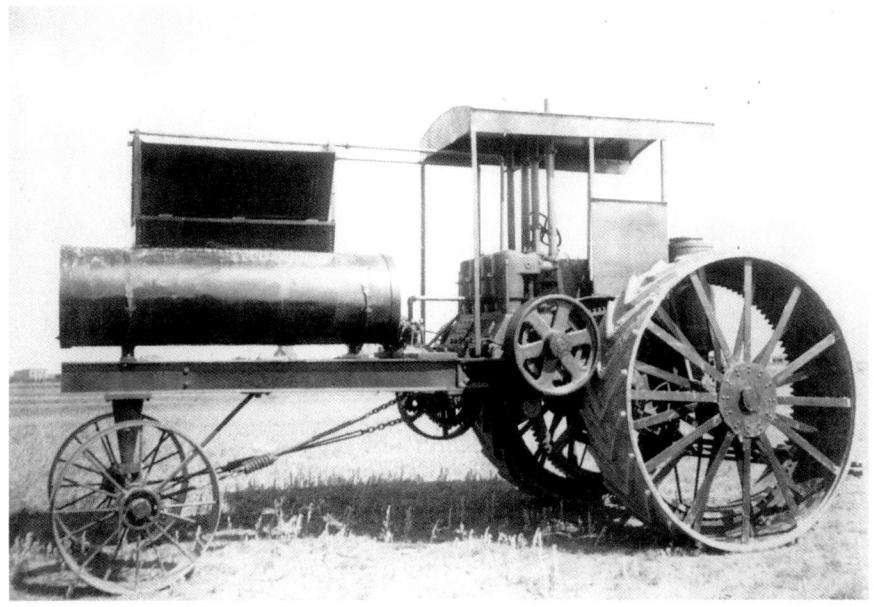

Colby Plow Boy Tractor—Jones Manufacturing. *Courtesy of Kansas State Historical Society.*

Manufacturing Company. This company was given the task of building the tractor. Under the direction of Jacob Bainter, the construction was accomplished by Meyers Jasperson, John McManis, H.D. Jones, John and Otto Spaeth and a tinsmith whose name is lost.

Three models were built in 1911, but disaster struck in the form of a severe drought that year. They were at the point that they could sell tractors, but the lack of capital prevented buyers from purchasing the tractors and putting them to work. The group did not have enough capital to sustain the process of building and marketing the tractor, as well as lasting through the depression of that time. As the article put it, "the dream came crashing down."

The group was forced to sell out, and the company and assets were purchased by Buffalo Pitt Company. This company later sold out to International Harvester Company. So the Plow Boy became the roots of the line of IHC tractors that is today Case-IH.

This spelled the end of Colby becoming a major manufacturing center for agricultural products. The Jones building was razed in 1965. The three tractors produced were sold, but no one knows where they ended up; it is likely that no Plow Boy survives to this day.

WACONDA SPRINGS

Waconda Springs was estimated by experts to be the only saltwater spring of its kind known in the world, and its history goes back millennia. The spring sat on the banks of the Solomon River and caused Senator Samuel C. Pomeroy (Kansas), when he toured the valley, to exclaim that the spring "was a most wonderful and a marvelous sight." The limestone walls that rose into the air were called a "crater of a volcano" by the senator. The minerals and salt that formed the walls rose about two hundred feet and had a perfectly round circumference.

Waconda Springs is located near Beloit and Cawker City. Native Americans from all over the region visited the springs for its healing powers. Waconda is from the Kanza word for "spiritual water" or "great spirit spring." The area was controlled by the Pawnee tribe, who called it *Pahowa* and *Kitzawitzuk*, which means "water on the bank." A geoglyph of a figure (formed by removing sod) is located on a hill about two miles southwest of the springs. The figure represents an unidentified animal, possibly a beaver. Soil analysis indicates that the figure is several hundred years old and has been maintained at least once after its original excavation.

The first recorded visit was by Lieutenant Zebulon Pike in his exploration of the Great Plains. Settlement in the area did not take place until after Kansas's statehood in 1861. The first settler in the area was a man named Pfeiffer, who took out the first claim on the property. After a few years, a man by the name of Burnham constructed a bottling works and began to sell the mineral water as a health tonic. He called it Waconda Flier.

An eastern investor named McWilliams decided to invest and built a stone sanitarium on the site. A building was completed ten years later, along with a hotel and health spa. In the 1890s, Waconda Flier was sold in all parts of the country and won a medal at the St. Louis World's Fair for its "superior medicinal qualities." The hotel and health spa passed through various owners and was improved; the facilities were modernized and offered physical therapy, hydro-therapy and dietary programs.

For hundreds of years, natives of the region came for the healing qualities of the water, and for more than fifty years, people came to "take the cure" from the springs. The Bureau of Reclamation decided that it was in the "interest of prosperity" to control the flooding of the Solomon River, and hence the Glenn Elder Dam was proposed. Resistance to the government coming in and building a lake over the historic site was fought long and hard. The project stalled until 1951, when Topeka, Lawrence and Kansas

City were devastated by floods. The furor over the flooding overtook any common sense solutions, such as possibly moving the dam upstream a few miles, and plans for the project were completed.

In 1953, geologist Walter H. Schoewe lamented that "Kansas can ill afford to destroy its historic, geologic, and scenic shrines." The state chamber of commerce endorsed a plan to designate the site as a monument to the American Indian. The fight was doomed because of the drought and flooding.

As a final insult, the sanatorium, hotel and all buildings on the site were bulldozed into the spring and Waconda Lake. Glenn Elder Dam now covers the marvel. One of the reasons given for the project besides flood control was irrigation. Since the construction of the lake, there has never been one drop of water used in irrigation.

The conditions in years since have made it almost impossible to destroy such a natural wonder. But the historic spring that was one of a kind in the world lies under the lake that is used for recreation and flood control.

ROYER TRACTORS

Royer Ensilage Harvester Company is shown in the *Standard Catalog of Farm Tractors, 1890–1980* as beginning in 1914 in Wichita. It lists the 12-25 Tractor in 1919 after incorporating as Royer Tractor Company. Not much is listed as known after that. But a combination of historical farm equipment enthusiasts and good luck reveals the story.

The first time the author discovered the Royer tractor story was at an antique tractor show and swap meet held annually by the Wheatland Poppin Johnnies Tractor Club. The meet was held at the Kansas Coliseum near Park City. At this particular show was a fully restored Royer tractor, one of only a few known to exist.

The next time the author was aware of the Royer was when it was featured in an issue of *Antique Power Magazine*. The story was of Ray Hoffman's interview with restorer and owner Jerry Abplanalp. The rescue of the Royer begins with a longtime collector and authority, Harold Ottaway. Harold's barns were filled to overflowing with old tractors and parts. Harold was known to go to any lengths to retrieve and save an old tractor, even going to South Dakota to retrieve an Emerson-Brantingham Big Four that had been submerged in a river.

Jerry Abplanalp owned a machine shop and did fabrication work for Ottaway on his projects when it was needed. After doing some work for Ottaway, Jerry was given the remains of a tractor that was rescued from a farmer's scrapheap near Anthony. That tractor turned out to be a Royer. It was around a 1918 or 1919 model, built in Wichita. Parts were scattered in three different barns.

The tractor was unique for the time in one major respect: it featured not only a friction drive but also a gear setup with driving chains on each side. The Royer was rated at twelve to twenty-five horsepower and operated on kerosene. It took eight years for Jerry to restore the tractor, which at the time was the only known example of the brand. It did have an Erd engine, which was used in several types of tractors during that time.

Pictures of the restoration shown in *Antique Power Magazine* show how painstaking the job was. The result, which this author witnessed at the show, was fabulous. One of the odd things about recovering all the parts for the restoration is that the flywheel was welded to a chain and served as Ottaway's mailbox post for many years.

In the research for this story, I was put into contact with Jerry Abplanalp's daughter, who was very excited that there was an interest in her father's project. Jerry is gone now, as is the Royer that created all the excitement when it was put up for sale. It is a shame that no one was able to purchase the Royer for display here in Kansas. The new owner proudly has the tractor displayed in a farm museum in Connecticut.

Royer manufactured its tractors at 315–17 West Waterman Street in Wichita. Advertising obtained from Jerry's daughter lists the Royer as being "A Maximum of Power, A Minimum of Parts." The sales brochure shows the tractor pulling a three-bottom plow and powering a threshing machine. An article written in *Old Iron Magazine* lists the model as a Royer D 12-25.

What became of the company is unknown. The tractor is listed as having been shown in the Kansas City Farm Show in 1920. It is reasonable to assume that after the farming boom of World War I, there was a slump and recession in farming in the 1920–22 period; it may be that the company could not survive the downturn.

During this time, it was the aspiration of many in the Wichita area to grow a large industrial base in aviation and agriculture. As with many dreams, some did not survive, but many who made the effort went on and did not let setbacks discourage them.

TYLER

As all larger metro areas grew, there were small towns and settlements that got absorbed and lost in time. Sometimes there is only a road name or something named for the place that managed to survive time, and maybe only those who live on these roads, or a part of an institution, know why the name exists. Tyler is one of those places.

As the Wichita & Western Railroad built west from Wichita, there were stations built every ten to twelve miles to not only provide water for the steam locomotives but also create business for the railroad and service for the settlers around these locations. The railroads made and broke many communities. Also, when populations grew and the diesel/electric trains displaced the need to stop so often, many communities just disappeared. The Wichita & Western became owned by the Santa Fe.

What is now Tyler Road in west Wichita is the only part of Tyler Station left to history. The intersection of what is now Harry Street and Tyler Road, just south of US 54/400 (aka Kellogg), was once the location of Tyler Station. The town was never platted or incorporated. There was an elevator (Coop) and a few houses. The Coop played a big role in the community.

One of the first mentions is in the 1903 *Wichita Beacon* due to a train derailment near Tyler Station. In the history of post offices, there is not one shown at Tyler, and yet the rural route carried Tyler addresses. In "Memories of Tyler," published in a neighborhood newsletter written by June Johnson, it is stated that the post office was closed prior to World War II.

The one thing known by most was the Tyler Cooperative Company elevator at that location. There was siding for loading grain cars and unloading freight. Richard Maus was the Coop manager from 1922 until 1954. Richard's son, Francis, recalled that the Coop sold coal, heating oil and battery radios. The Coop store sold much more. The author's family purchased a TV, GE mixer and other small appliances from the store.

The houses that were built near Tyler were mostly for Coop employees. Children went to Daisy School, one mile west on Harry. In later years, Tyler Road, which intersected with the original US Highway 54 and is now Maple Street (aka the Old Cannonball), was paved on the west half only so loaded grain trucks would be on a hard surface while waiting to dump grain at the elevator during harvest.

There was an unusual house across the street from the Coop that was bought by Joe Brady. Joe and Cathleen raised seven children there and started the first nursery in the Wichita area; Joe had a degree in horticulture.

Kansas Oddities

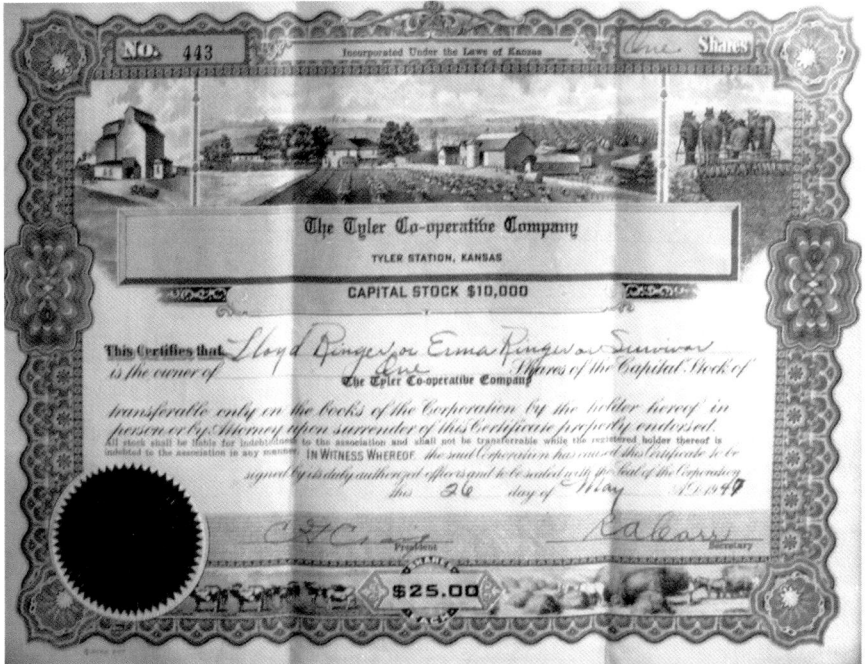

Tyler stock certificate. *Photo by Roger Ringer.*

The family business is still operating, located west of Maize Road off US 54/400 (Kellogg), just one and a half miles from the original Tyler homesite.

Tyler Cooperative was incorporated with capital stock of $10,000. One share cost $25. The author's grandparents on both sides were charter members of the Tyler Coop. Lloyd and Erma Ringer bought one share on May 26, 1947. Grandfather Carl Becker was a charter member. The Coop closed in 1954.

Richard Maus and his sons built an appliance and hardware store north of the Coop at what would be Kellogg and Tyler Road, called Maus Supply. It would be an institution in the area for many years. Other residents for many years were the Zandlers. After the Coop closed, a lumber yard (that burned down) was at the site.

Over the ensuing years, the Callahan and Westport additions were built. On January 1, 1955, the Sedgwick County Fire District No. 1 opened Station 3 one mile north (at Tyler and University). At that time, the west Wichita city limits were five miles east on West Street. Both housing developments were annexed into Wichita in the 1970s.

Memories of Tyler still live within a few old residents and families, although most Sedgwick County residents will never know why that street is called Tyler Road.

JOHN DAVID JORDAN: FREEPORT

John Jordan was born in Wellington, Kansas, on May 18, 1927, and lived with his family on a farm one mile north of Freeport in Harper County. His parents, Neal and Mildred, raised John and farmed on the property. Upon graduation from Harper High School, John and all the boys from the class went to the recruiting office and joined the U.S. Navy. John was trained on and operated landing craft, was involved in many of the island invasions in the Pacific Theater and was under fire quite a bit of the time. Driving LSTs probably led to his later love of motorboat racing. John was being held in ready status for the invasion of Japan when the atomic bombs were dropped, ending the war. He was sent back to San Diego until his discharge.

Upon returning home, John attended Kansas State University and came home during the summers to farm with his dad. While at K-State, he met a girl named Pat Dodds from the Riley County area and soon married her. There were several who raced hydroplane boats in the area around Manhattan, and John was soon racing locally. As his skills improved, he entered regional and national races and was soon winning top honors.

One of John's good friends was Max Blue, who was building aluminum fishing boats at Goddard, Kansas. One time, as John was racing at Lake Afton, Max came down and looked at the hydroplane boats and told John that he believed he could build the boat style out of aircraft aluminum like his fishing boats. John told him that would be a great idea, but his ideas on improving the boat would also give it an edge in competition. Max built the boat that John had specified to him and was soon turning the heads of the entire boating world. The popular idea was that nothing could outperform the fiberglass boats that dominated the sport.

Not only was John turning heads in motorboat racing, but so was his wife, Pat. John was winning Class B but was too heavy to be able to race in Class A hydroplanes. So, Pat took control and won with the new Blue Star boats. Soon racing was their main interest (and farming was not what John wanted to do).

Back on the farm, John's father, Neal, was a wheat and dairy farmer and wanted his only son to take over and carry on the farm. But John's heart was not in farming. John and Pat were best friends with neighbors Milford and Pat Coady. When Neal decided to sell the farm, the Coadys bought it, and the family still lives there as of this publication. Neal was elected to a term in the Kansas legislature, and John and Pat moved to Haysville.

John went to work for Mercury Outboard Motors (whose products he had been using on his boats). John and Pat had four children. The German motor company Koening sent John motors to use in his racing, and they soon put him into the winning circles. By going to work for Mercury, he would be ensured a regular income, but this meant the family had to move to West Monroe, Louisiana. John was soon traveling so much it was hard to have a family life. In order to settle down and be able to be home all the time, John and Pat created their own business.

John and Pat created Jordan's Saw and Marina, combining several dealerships that included Bultaco Motorcycles in West Monroe. One of their sons was an active motocross racer. The business expanded to the point that they were too busy to have much free time, so they put the business up for sale. After the sale, the couple spent several years traveling and had a highlight of spending three months in Alaska.

In John's retirement years, he worked with Electrolux, enjoying traveling and visiting with people. In the last years, John was affected by Alzheimer's and died on June 8, 2015. He is buried at the Freeport Cemetery. Many friends and relatives live in the Harper area.

John David Jordan was an innovator and with his wife enjoyed life and raised a family. It seems odd to say "farmer" and "champion motorboat racer" in the same sentence, yet this is one more example of a Kansan with a dream.

ROCKEFELLER RANCH: FRANK ROCKEFELLER

In the southeast corner of Kiowa County, right behind what remains of Belvidere, was the headquarters of Frank Rockefeller's Soldier Creek Ranch. The ranch, variously described as from five thousand to thirteen thousand acres, was a showcase owned by the youngest brother of oil tycoon John D. Rockefeller.

Franklin "Frank" Rockefeller and his twin sister, Francis, born on August 8, 1845, in Richford, New York, were the youngest children of William Avery "Bill" Rockefeller. The family moved to Cleveland, Ohio, where his father pursued his business interests. Many historians and documents refer to Bill as a con artist. Frank's two older brothers, John D. and William Jr., owned Standard Oil Company.

Though underage, Frank joined the Seventh Ohio Infantry in September 1861. His Civil War service saw him in the battles of Winchester, Port Republic, Cedar Mountain, Chancellorsville, Gettysburg, Lookout Mountain and others, including Sherman's March to Atlanta. At Chancellorsville, Frank was wounded in the head by grapeshot.

After his service, he pursued business ventures and eventually joined his brothers in the oil business, rising to vice-president at Standard Oil. He had a falling out with his brother John that lasted the rest of his life. He also had an interest in Pioneer Oil Company. As one of his interests, Frank bought the ranch at Belvidere. He also bought two ranches in northwest Kansas in Rawlins and Cheyenne Counties.

The ranch at Belvidere was located on Soldier Creek and was in the area of the headwaters of the Medicine River, Spring Creek, Tertiary Springs and Thompson Creek. Besides the deeded acreage, the strength of the ranch lay in open range and a lack of settlers. The ranch raised Hereford and shorthorn cattle and buffalo. Frank was sensitive about being referred to as a "millionaire" and being called a "hobby rancher," so in 1901 he was elected to the presidency of the Hereford Breeders Association. He also bought the best bull in the world and brought him to the ranch. Columbus XVII was purchased for $5,050. The bull was born and raised in England on the farm of Queen Victoria. He also made a donation of a calf to the Kansas State Agricultural College.

Five hundred acres of alfalfa were raised on the ranch for feed. The ranch house was a New England style with a fireplace, a library, a study, many bedrooms, running water, heat and a tennis court. Many parties were held at the ranch over the years. Frank actually fitted the rancher type, as he was five feet, eleven inches tall and weighed two hundred pounds. He was plain-spoken and did not give the impression of being a millionaire. He was quoted by the *Wichita Eagle* as describing his ranch as "his piece of heaven on earth."

He was a firm believer in hornless cattle. There were fifteen large barns on the property. He employed many men to manage and operate the ranch and his other ranches in northwest Kansas. When the Santa Fe Railroad came through Belvidere, it spelled the end of the open range by bringing many settlers in to take homesteads and build fences.

In Rawlins County, Frank became involved in a dispute with neighbor Chancey Dewey. Dewey sent five men with Winchesters and pistols to cut wire and graze on Frank's land. Dewey was charged and convicted. Dewey would end up being involved in the Dewey Berry Feud. In 1905, Frank sold his western Kansas ranches. By 1915, the buffalo were all sold. Frank died two years later, leaving a wife and three daughters. The next year, the cattle were sold to the highest bidder.

Although it seemed Frank did not forgive or have contact with his two brothers, they both came to his funeral. The legacy of the Rockefeller Ranch is an interesting part of Kansas history, and the basic ranch still runs today. But that is another story.

RALPH K. ODOR: VORNADO AIRPLANE

Ralph Odor was born on April 5, 1895, on a farm near Arcadia, Oklahoma. He was the son of a man with vision and inventiveness. His father, William H. Odor, built a round barn that is a landmark in the Arcadia area and long supported his son's ventures. Ralph served in World War I and was a trombonist for the Great Lakes Navy Band under the direction of John Philip Sousa.

Ralph became an engineer and inventor, and his work after the war led him to travel on many airplanes. During this time, he started to imagine new ways to create propulsion for an aircraft, and his rough designs led to a new style of aircraft. He returned to the Arcadia area and developed the theory that was called a "vortex tornado." Using the concept of how a tornado works, he designed an engine and propelling system that brought air into a tube structure, creating the same vortex effect as a tornado.

Combining *vortex* and *tornado* to create the name "Vornado," he built models of the concept for a Vornado plane. Ralph landed a position at Oklahoma A&M University (Oklahoma State), and work on the airplane continued through the 1920s. The prototype flew tethered in 1929, powered by electric motors, making the Vornado airplane prototype the first airplane to be powered by electricity.

A man in Italy named Luigi Stipa is given credit in most circles for creating the first airplane with an intubed propeller. This "first" airplane was built in 1932 and was named the Stipa-Carproni. However, the first video of the flight of the Vornado prototype was shot in 1929 and can be seen on YouTube today.

An invitation and an agreement with Oklahoma A&M provided a laboratory, materials and students to work on the Vornado projects. The agreement was that Ralph would retain patent rights to what came from his research, but the college would profit by the results of Ralph's work. A report issued in June 1935 noted the progress of the project by the Oklahoma A&M College, Division of Engineering. The report contained the design of the propeller structure as patented and the design of a twin-engine Vornado-powered airplane. This was all made possible by invitation of Colonel Phillip S. Donnell, dean of engineering, at Oklahoma A&M experiment station.

The first patent application for the Vornado airplane was attempted in 1931 through a patent attorney in Oklahoma City. However, there was a failing in the engineering related to this first application, and work began on a new application. The new application was finally filed on July 31, 1934, and granted in 1938. In 1935, the Vornado Trust was formed to receive, own and control all patents and applications it owned, and it was the trust that disbursed all income.

In 1938, the airplane was put on the shelf, and the focus shifted to the production of fans and air circulation systems. In 1936, Ralph went to Philadelphia to work with patent attorneys. The development and testing of the Vornado principles shifted focus from aircraft to the fans during this time. Ralph became affiliated with a man by the name of Kern Dodge on his patents and designs. Dodge became a board member of the Vornado Trust.

In 1938 and 1939, Ralph developed the "rigid spinning" of metal fabrication method. This was done to quiet the noise of the flanges in the designs and was used in cowling production for aircraft engines. In 1939, a deal was made with Propellair in Ohio to manufacture two sizes of a fan based on Ralph's design. Only a few fans were manufactured under the Propellair name before World War II intervened and cut supplies.

In 1940, Ralph went to Wright-Patterson Air Base and was directed to Wichita, where he was hired by Aircraft Welders Company. This company was owned by O.A. Sutton. Ralph went to work designing cowlings and various types of motor mounts. He also patented a design for a lounge chair.

In a newspaper story of December 4, 1936, from the *Daily Capital News* (Jefferson City, Missouri), Ralph talked about the design for a full-size Vornado airplane as a "space ship." He expressed that the new engines would create terrific power. If built, the airplane was estimated to be able to fly ten thousand miles before refueling. If the plane had been built, Oklahoma test pilot Roy Hunt was supposed to be the first to fly it. It was never built, so we will never know if it would have changed aviation.

But there is more to the story.

VORNADO

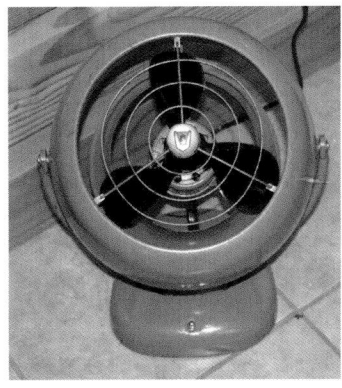

Vornado Fan. *Photo by Roger Ringer.*

The first fans and air circulation system devices were built by Propellair in Ohio, but that production was limited by the onset of World War II. Ralph Odor ended up in Wichita working as an engineer for the O.A. Sutton Company, which was doing aircraft work with Beechcraft and other companies. As the production of war materials was evaporating, new areas were needed to keep the Sutton Company running, so the decision was made to produce the Vornado Fan.

Conflict soon arose between Ralph and Sutton when credit for the design was not given for the Vornado Fan. In the meantime, the advent of air conditioning was putting fans on the road to the museum. As envisioned, fans would only be used to supplement air conditioning in places where it was not feasible to install air conditioning.

When Ralph left Sutton and went back to Oklahoma, a person was brought in who soon was given full credit for the design of the Vornado Fan—thereafter perpetuated by a local business paper. After much discussion, the credit was restored to Ralph as being the inventor.

The Vornado Trust soon sold all patents on the designs and invested in real estate, becoming one of the largest real estate trusts in the nation. The Sutton Company had moved into coiled air conditioning systems and sold that division to Amana Corporation. The company started to shut down in 1958, and in 1959, the O.A. Sutton Company was purchased by the Two Guys Discount Department Store chain. Not long after, the Vornado brand lay dormant.

In 1989, the Vornado Air Circulation Company was founded by Michael Croup, a collector and restorer of Vornado Fans. The company was started in Andover. The designs were improved, and whole room circulators were developed. The company has done extensive research on the original Vornado design and developed new designs with new materials.

In December 2006, the company was sold to a private equity firm and renamed Vornado Air LLC. The Omaha-based McCarthy Capital group led the acquisition and had plans to take annual sales from tens of millions to hundreds of millions in the first five years. The company does not disclose numbers, so the actual increase achieved is not known.

The story of the company and Ralph Odor was not fully known to the new owners, and the unraveling of the Vornado story was a revelation for them. Because of patent takeovers and disputes between O.A. Sutton and Ralph Odor, as well as the workings of a design engineer named Ten Eyck, the story had gotten jumbled up.

The story was straightened out by Ralph's grandson, Don Morris, who had inherited his grandfather's papers, news clippings and video. The clouded history of the Vornado was cleared up, and Mr. Morris is publishing a biography on Ralph.

The company is still a leader in airflow technology, and the product is still built in Andover, Kansas. The company continued to expand through the recession of the 2010s, and Vornado continues to be a highly collected and useable fan—another inventor's dream in which Kansas played a large role.

ACE AIRCRAFT COMPANY: KANSAS LEGACY

Orland George Corben was born in Des Moines, Iowa. He learned to fly in a World War I surplus Curtis JN4 "Jenny" in 1918. He barnstormed around the Midwest and filmed aerial footage for newsreel producers in between performing in the flying circuses.

Corben started designing aircraft in the mid-1920s. He believed that aviation should be safe, easy, fun and available at an inexpensive price. He ended up in Wichita and in 1929 created the Ace Aircraft Company. At the time, there were fifty-three aviation and aviation-related companies in Wichita. Wichita earned the name "Air Capital" by being the center of the independent fledgling aviation business.

The first plane that Corben designed and built was the Baby Ace. The first motor was a Heath Henderson modified motorcycle engine. The Baby Ace was built and sold as a kit plane. Operations were set up at 1016 South Santa Fe. The company was started in 1929 and was listed in the companies that went defunct in 1930. The Wall Street crash of 1929 had the effect of killing the majority of aviation nationwide. Ace became one of those victims.

The Baby Ace design, however, was solid, and Corben moved to Madison, Wisconsin, in 1931. There he created the Corben Sport Plane Company, while also designing the Junior Ace, a two-seater. He had designed a prototype known as the Super Ace. Yet even here the Great Depression overtook the company. Leaving for other aviation interests, Corben left all his drawings, parts and inventory in the hangar in Wisconsin. In 1953, Paul Proberezny acquired all Corben materials.

Proberezny was one of the founders of the Experimental Aircraft Association. He was approached by *Mechanics Illustrated* magazine to do a series of articles on building aircraft at home. There was a demand for plans that were generated by this. He felt that as a founding member and administrator of the EAA, this would become a conflict of interest. The company rights were sold to Edwin T. Jacob of McFarland, Wisconsin, in 1961. Since then, the rights have passed through several hands.

The current owner is Bill Woods of Toccoa, Georgia. The company is headquartered at Toccoa, and there is a website where kits for the Baby Ace, Ace Junior and Ace Scooter can be purchased.

The aircraft industry has always been a topsy-turvy proposition. Kansas is fertile soil for dreamers. Those willing to pursue a dream and establish a business have created a long line of these kinds of ventures. It is good to know that sometimes good ideas can be raised from the ashes and reinvented.

DEAD COW INTERNATIONAL

If you have ever come into Wichita on K-42 highway and noticed airplanes taking off and landing to the south, it may start you wondering. The intersection of K-42 and West Street is also the intersection with Pawnee. Travel a block or two east on Pawnee and you will see the sign for Dead Cow International.

The story goes back long before there was an Eisenhower (Mid Continent) Airport. It actually was located there when the airport was located where McConnell AFB and Boeing are located. Earl Long is the owner as of the writing of this book. His father was also named Earl.

The Long family farm was located on the south and east side of what is now Pawnee and West Streets. Mr. Long was a pilot and had bought an air service at the old Wichita Airport. Mr. Long believed that aviation was the wave of the future and built Westport Airport on his farm. One of the famous things about the airstrip was the fact that many times the cattle would be on the runway and a pilot would have to buzz the strip to run the livestock off before he could land.

Of course, this led to the incident that gave the airport its unofficial name, Dead Cow International. One night, a pilot flying a Fairchild PT-19 landed, hitting something in the process. The next day, Mr. Long asked, "Who was flying the airplane that hit the cow and killed it?" The story varies with the tellers, but the good-natured kidding that resulted from the incident resulted in the airport being called Dead Cow International.

Mr. and Mrs. Long went through a divorce in the 1970s, and Mrs. Long offered the business to her two sons. One son got tired of being poor and left to get a job. Earl did earn degrees in math and physics from Friends University and a master's degree from New Mexico Institute of Mining Technology. He spent ten years at Boeing Wichita as a test engineer, spending most of his time in the B-52 program. He was involved in other programs at Boeing, and he earned his pilot's license as well.

The airport is still in operation and has several hangars and maintenance facilities. The company does major airframe and engine maintenance. It is also the home of the Kansas Chapter of the Commemorative Air Force. There is a Cessna 150 for rent and a lot of stories that get swapped by the patrons who come and go on a daily basis.

KANSAS SUNFLOWER

Kansas is best known as the Sunflower State. What is not well known is how that name became official. Sunflowers have been considered pests and weeds by many in the past and present. It is a common prairie flower that Nebraska also considered adopting as its state flower.

In fact, when this bill was being considered, there was opposition to it from State Representative Frank Martin, who opposed the designation by saying, "That weed is in many respects worse than a cocklebur." Ten years prior to the adoption of the sunflower as the state flower, there was a bill to declare it a noxious weed to be eradicated.

In fact, it was the people of the state of Kansas who started using the sunflower as a symbol of the state before it was so designated officially by the Kansas legislature. Senator George Morehouse from Council Grove was attending a rodeo in Colorado Springs and noticed that the Kansas people wore sunflower buttons on their vests identifying them as being from Kansas. He was impressed by the idea and inspired to introduce a bill for the official designation of the sunflower as the official flower of Kansas.

In the original bill, Senator Morehouse stated that "this flower has to all Kansans a historic symbolism which speaks of frontier days, winding trails, pathless prairie, and is full of glory of the past, the pride of the present, richly emblematic of the golden future, and is a flower which has given Kansas the world wide name 'The Sunflower State.'"

The bill was drafted in 1903 and signed into law on March 12, 1903. Later that year, Governor Willis Bailey ordered the uniform of the state militia to reflect the new symbol. The collar device of the full dress, dress

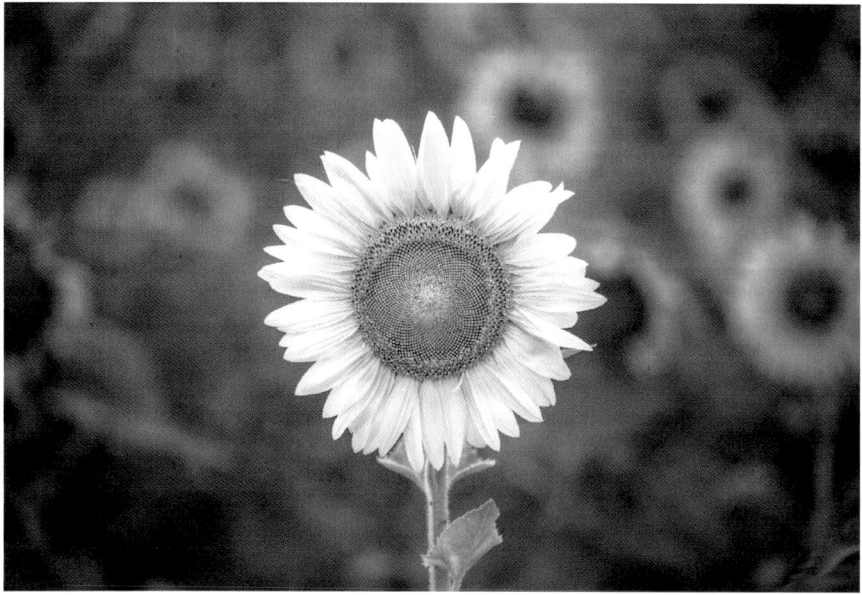

The sunflower, state flower of Kansas. *Photo by Matt Palmer.*

and service coats of officers and enlisted men of the Kansas National Guard is the sunflower.

In 1919, Albert T. Reid was asked to submit a design for a state flag on a blue field with a sunflower centered. The modified version was adopted with the blue field and the seal of the state and a bar centered with a sunflower that symbolized the Louisiana Purchase.

Alf Landon used the sunflower prominently on his campaign buttons and materials in his run for president of the United States.

The domesticated sunflower has become an important agricultural commodity for the state. Sunflower oil is a healthy vegetable oil, the seeds are healthy snacks and the seeds are added as a nutritious ingredient in many foods.

Ode to the Sunflower
Oh sunflower! The queen of all flowers,
No other with you can compare,
The roadside and fields made golden,
Because of your bright presence there.
—Ed Blair, 1901

HAMMTOWN: NORMAN HAMM

Norman Hamm bought a steel-wheeled tractor in 1939 and went on the road custom-cutting wheat. Hamm was from Perry, Kansas, and his favorite saying was, "Right is Right and Wrong is Wrong." It seems that everyone who had contact with him remembers his way of doing business and handling people.

Hammtown was founded in 1939, and by the end of the custom cutting business, his was the largest one-owner custom cutting crew on the road. Kids who worked for him in 1961 recalled that there were ten Massey-Ferguson combines and ten Chevy two-ton trucks. There were twenty men hired. Those with farm experience drove the combines, and the others drove the trucks to the bins and elevators.

To support the twenty-man crew, there were bunkhouses made from truck and bus bodies and a dining trailer with a kitchen that would feed fourteen at a time—pulled by a truck with a water tank, a generator, a freezer and supplies. There were also shower and laundry facilities. All equipment,

Kansas Oddities

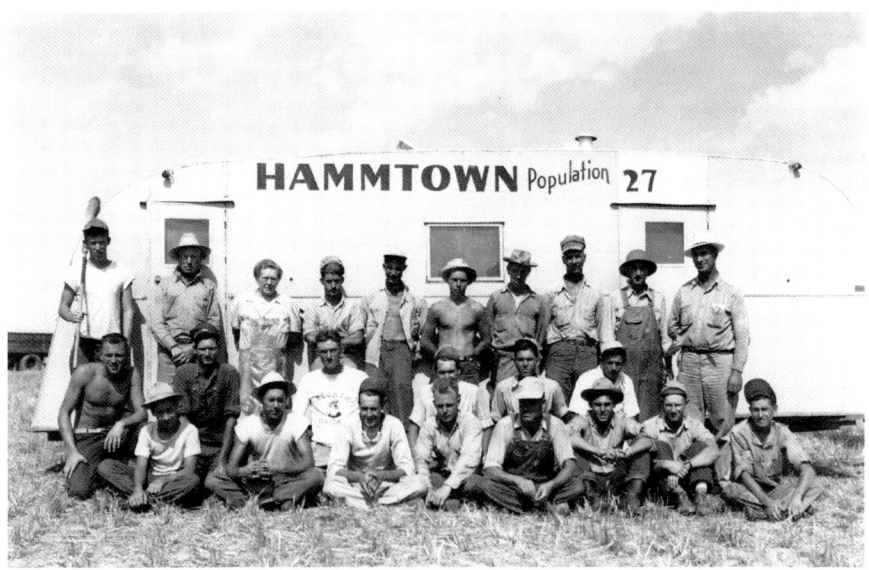

Hammtown custom cutting crew setting off on the harvest. *Courtesy of Kansas State Historical Society.*

except the combines, was painted blue with white tops. On the road, they ate in restaurants.

The departure of the custom crews was a big deal in those days, and on several occasions the governor of the state came to send them off. The first stop in Texas was the Waggoner Ranch, which is the largest ranch in the country under one fence and second only to the King Ranch in acreage (also in Texas). The Waggoner Ranch was sold in 2015 to a California buyer.

The Hammtown crew followed the harvest north into the Dakotas before returning home. With the many contracts that Norman had from the custom cutting business, he became the first in Kansas to buy a bulldozer and build ponds and lakes for farmers. Always looking for opportunities, he bought eighty acres to farm at US 24 and US 59 highways near Perry. There was a deposit of rock on the property, and he started to mine and sell rock. This expanded the company from the custom cutting days into a large construction business.

It is not an uncommon sight to see Hamm equipment on highway projects all over the state. In the 1950s, Hamm established Norman Hamm Inc. and N.R. Hamm Quarry. Along the way, he purchased other companies and diversified. He created Hamm's Municipal Solid Waste Landfill, which serves Lawrence, Topeka and other northeast Kansas communities.

Today, the company is employee-owned, and the third generation of Hamm's still manages and works for the businesses. Always known as a common man, Norman was considered someone who could communicate with anyone. He served as mayor of Perry and while on the board graded and rocked all the alleys in town and never billed the city. He considered it something that needed to be done. He was a member of the Perry Lions Club, board member of the Kaw Valley Bank and on the Kansas Contractors Association Board of Directors. He gave $150,000 toward the construction of the Lawrence Arts Center; he was its largest donor.

Norman Hamm was born on May 23, 1911, in the Buck Creek Community near Williamstown. He died on August 4, 2003, at Lawrence.

THE FLEAGLE GANG

The Fleagle Gang probably stole more money than any gang in the 1920s. Some estimate that the Fleagles were responsible for 60 percent of the bank robberies in the 1920s. There are many who have the notoriety—like Bonnie and Clyde, Baby Face Nelson, Machine Gun Kelly, John Dillinger and the Barker Gang—but not the Fleagles. Many of the robberies that they committed were not known because their robberies were covered up to keep public confidence in the local institutions.

The Fleagle family moved from Iowa to western Kansas in the 1880s. Their farm was northwest of Garden City and became the center of the gang's activities for several years. Ralph was born in 1880 and Jake in 1890; there were two other boys who stayed straight and did not join the brothers' life of crime. That did not mean that the family did not benefit from Ralph and Jake's business enterprises.

Neighbors noticed that Ralph and Jake came and went often. The family was also prospering with not much evidence of actual farming or ranching going on. Locally, the ranch was known as the "no horse horse ranch." There was a new house built and a new tractor bought. The two put the story to the family and the neighbors that they were successful stockbrokers and made a fortune in the markets. There were large cash deposits in banks around the state, and the bills and purchases were paid for with large-denomination bills.

What the boys were doing was going to the West Coast and robbing high-stakes poker and craps games. These robberies were not reported to authorities. At some point, the gang started to rob banks. Banks in the Midwest and on the West Coast were robbed with some success, and up until the heist in Lamar, Colorado, they had not used their guns. Banks in Kinsley, Larned and many other towns were taken for large amounts of money plus bearer bonds.

There is one thing that was a first. It was the first time that a crime had been solved with the use of fingerprints. This was thanks to an early arrest and one-year imprisonment of Jake in the Oklahoma State Penitentiary. Jake was arrested under an alias in California but gained release by having an alibi for the charge at the time. The local police sent the fingerprint to the Bureau of Investigation, which would eventually become the Federal Bureau of Investigation. A single fingerprint on the car belonging to a doctor who had been murdered and dumped in a ravine, along with his car, after the Lamar holdup would be the undoing of the gang.

At Lamar, Colorado, a heist was planned for the First National Bank. Working alongside the brothers were George Abshier from Colorado and Howard Royston from California. The brothers had rented another place not far from their parents' farm so they could plan their robberies more securely. On the day of the heist, they entered the bank, filling their sacks with $220,000 worth of cash and bonds. The streak of not using their guns ended when the bank president pulled a .45 pistol from his desk and fired, hitting Royston in the jaw. The banker, A.N. Parish, was immediately killed. (A side note: Mr. Parish's pistol had been given to him by Frank James the year before. It is ironic that the pistol used to try and stop the robbery had belonged to one of the most notorious robbers of all time.)

The gang grabbed the banker's son, J.N. Parish, and another employee, Ed Lungren, as hostages. Ralph was very methodical when planning a robbery and had learned all the roads in the counties so the getaway was never on main roads. The sheriff was close behind them on their way out of town, and they shot the radiator of his car, disabling it. Once outside of town, they dropped off Lungren, driving back to Kansas by back roads. Needing a doctor for Royston, Dr. W.W. Wineieger was lured out, thinking that a boy had his foot caught in a tractor. The doctor never returned and was found days later by an airplane from the Colorado National Guard, shot in the back of his Hudson car, which had been left out in the country. He was tied and gagged, but that is where the mistake was made. The car had been wiped down for fingerprints, but one print was found. It was a long shot, but the persistence of one officer and the arrest in California eventually led to identifying the owner of the fingerprint as Jake Fleagle.

The gang split up, but the sheriff found a letter at the Fleagle home giving away the fact that Ralph was living in Illinois. Ralph was arrested in Kankakee and brought back to Garden City. Then he made a deal to talk if they would not ask for the death penalty. Royston was arrested in San Andreas, California. Royston gave up Abshier, and all three were convicted despite the plea deal. Ralph was hanged, as were the other two, at Canon City, Colorado. Jake disappeared and after living in Missouri was shot during his arrest at Branson, Missouri, dying shortly afterward.

ROBBERY AT FARMERS & DROVERS BANK

On March 2, 1926, the Fleagle Gang robbed the Farmers & Drovers Bank at Council Grove. The first clue as to who pulled the bank job was the blue Buick that the gang preferred as a getaway car. The bank employees were herded into the vault, with the robbers not knowing that there was a telephone in the vault, which the employees used to call the Sheriff's Office. At the same time, Clarence White was returning from a meeting, and as he entered the front door of the bank, he could tell something was not right. He ran across the street to the hardware store to alert the local vigilante committee.

During this time, there was no state law enforcement group, and each county was stopped by jurisdictional lines. The Kansas Bankers Association and the state sent guns to towns that organized vigilante groups to guard against bank robbery. As the robbers started to leave town, the group at the hardware store thought that the rifles sent were too dangerous to fire in town. By the time they swapped the rifles for shotguns and found shells, only a few shots were sent toward the blue Buick. The paper at the time criticized the group for poor marksmanship.

The call went out immediately. All the main roads were blocked, and people were sure that the robbers would be stopped. The Fleagle Gang, however, always learned the back roads and most unlikely routes for their getaways. The cars were spotted in several locations, but the robbers got away clean.

It was thought that the gang would be headed toward Wichita, but police found the stolen blue Buick several days later parked in Kansas City. The insurance company had already settled with the owner of the car, so the insurance adjuster drove the car back to Council Grove later during the investigation.

The take for the heist was determined to be $5,000. The Fleagles were never prosecuted for the robbery. Two years later, the gang robbed the bank in Lamar, Colorado, which would be the undoing of the gang. An interesting note about the Fleagles is that they not only spent the money but also banked a lot in locations around the Midwest. They were also notorious for burying their loot in many locations. Three caches have been unearthed in three states so far, and speculation is that there is more. It was claimed by the family that all the buried money on the family farm had been dug up and banked.

After ninety years, one day some visitors to the museum in Council Grove remarked that their family was in the scrapbook kept there. Upon being asked what family, they replied "the Fleagle family." When asked what relationship they had to Jake Fleagle, they replied, "We don't really know for sure, 'cause Grampa never wanted to talk about it."

BANK ASSOCIATION VIGILANTES

The famous headlines and names that capture the attention of the movies and historians about the bank robbers of the 1920s and '30s may give you the impression that these were the most notorious headliners. But they weren't. The end of World War I brought an end to high commodity prices, and there was a recession in the country. By 1920, things were starting to move back up, and the Roaring Twenties was the result. By the time the effects of the crash on Wall Street were felt and the Great Depression set in, the incidence of bank robberies skyrocketed.

Public opinion was not always on the banker's side. In frontier days and the time before insurance, robbing a bank was robbing each individual who had money in the bank. After the offering of insurance, the personal bite from a bank robbery was removed for the ordinary person.

Movies and even history books leave the impression with the general public that there was a tie-in with organized crime on many bank robberies. This was just not the case. The majority of bank robbers were individuals, and their gangs were a scourge on the small-town banks. Kansas homegrown robbers like the Fleagle Gang and Eddie Adams were desperate characters who robbed across a multistate area.

In the 1920s and 1930s, two-thirds of the bank robberies, both daylight and burglary, happened in eight states. Indiana bankers lost more than

$1 million in the 1920s alone. The states of California, Illinois, Indiana, Kansas, Michigan, Missouri, Oklahoma and Texas bore the largest brunt of the robberies during this twenty-year period.

Kansas was no different than other states in the fact that the insurance companies that paid the losses were paying out 123 percent of the premiums collected. Some banks were content to not oppose the robbers and let the insurance companies take the hit. It was a fact that insurance would not be available very long at that rate of loss. Also, there was a fear for the safety of employees and customers when these robberies occurred.

There was no statewide law enforcement agency at this time, and it was only toward the end of the 1930s that the FBI came into its own and became effective enough to go after bank robbers. The law enforcement of the day was very lacking, with no training, poor equipment and no authority to cross jurisdictional lines. The Bankers Associations in these states advocated a system of vigilantes that would be organized locally and under the authority of the county sheriff. These vigilantes would be different from the classic image of the vigilante groups that took the law into their own hands and meted out justice as they saw fit. These vigilantes were armed by the bankers associations with rifles, pistols and shotguns, many of which came from military stocks.

There were organized events and training sessions, such as the three hundred vigilantes from seventy counties that went to Fort Riley on September 12, 1927. They spent the night in tents, rose to the sound of the bugle, ate an army breakfast and went to the range for their annual target practice. While at Fort Riley, they were given a talk by Brigadier General Charles Symmonds, attended a horse show and watched a boxing match. There are many stories of actions taken by citizens during and after bank robberies, as well as of the success and non-success that they had. The point was to not only thwart the robbery but also to call ahead to neighboring towns for roadblocks and, in some cases, even put up airplanes to try and track the robbers.

Just such an action was taken at Garden Plain when Eddie Adams and his gang broke into the store at Cullison. The Pratt County Sheriff's Office called C.L. Wulf to set up a roadblock on the Cannonball Highway to try to apprehend the fugitives. Along with W.E. Mouldin and R.H. Gosney, they blocked the bridge over Polecat Creek. Carl Wiske and Charles Self were roused, and the four mounted in the Page trouble car from Wulf Garage and blocked the bridge in the west side of town. They also called Mr. Gosney near Goddard to set up a roadblock in case they got past the Garden Plain group.

The group parked the Page on the bridge, blocking it completely, and waited for the gang. In a few minutes, the Buick touring car approached at a high rate of speed. It ran into the Page, demolishing it. The Buick was badly damaged and went into the ditch. One man armed with a Colt automatic pistol fell out and dropped his gun. He was captured immediately. The other man took off running, not heeding the shouts to stop or the four shots fired in his direction.

The captured man was put in the Garden Plain lockup. Getting a new car, the group started out after the other robber. One mile north of town, the group looked under a bridge and failed to see the man hiding up in the stringers, but on a second pass, they noticed his legs hanging down. The Sedgwick County sheriff came and took the prisoners, the money and the Buick back to the Pratt County Jail.

Later on, the robber Eddie Adams broke out of prison and was killed in a shootout with police. The other man who had broken out had come to Wichita and was on his way to Garden Plain to make good on his threat to kill Mr. Wulf. He was recognized and killed in a shootout in Wichita, much to the relief of Mr. Wulf, who was a bit nervous when told about the jailbreak.

In Kansas, as result of the high incidence of robberies and the loss of citizens' and police officers' lives, the Kansas Bureau of Investigation was created. Most other states created state police or investigative agencies to deal with the problems of jurisdictional lines and the implementation of scientific law enforcement techniques. There were also changes in laws, increased training and better equipment advocated.

There were still banks in many towns up into the 1950s and '60s that had firearms from the vigilante program on their premises. Rifles were used in a bank robbery in Cheney years after the war when a banker's son and a customer chased robbers at high speed for miles. The robbers were apprehended near Anthony because the tenacious pair would stop along the way and call the location in as they pursued the robbers. After the hair-raising ride the banker's son had, with the customer driving, he swore he would not do that again.

EDWARD "EDDIE" ADAMS: BANK ROBBER

One of the most notorious bank robbers to escape attention of the movies was Eddie Adams. Eddie was born in or near Hutchinson (records are sketchy on this) in 1887. His birth name is listed as William Joseph Wallace. His father died, and his mother remarried when he was young. He did not like his stepfather, and it is noted that he was not fond of physical labor. He took up the barber trade and moved to Wichita sometime after 1900. He met a man named John Callahan and soon was involved in bootlegging, petty robberies and car theft.

It is not known who he married or when he married, but his charismatic personality attracted many hangers-on and attractive women. Tiring of his infidelity and criminal activities, his wife left him. Forming his own gang, he moved up to train robberies and bank robberies throughout Kansas, Missouri and Iowa. In 1920, he moved up (or down) to murder. Forming a partnership with the Major brothers, Ray and Walter, on September 5, 1920, they attempted a daylight robbery against a Kansas City gambling den on Grand Avenue owned by Harry Trusdell.

The illegal gambling den was a tough place with tough employees, and a gun battle ensued, killing gambler and gunman Frank Gardner. This led to the rest of them being captured by police. Adams was sentenced to life, and the Major brothers took a plea deal and received five years. While being transported to the Missouri State Prison, Adams made a break, jumping from the train. A few days later, he was involved in the robbery of a general store in Cullison and the bank. Calling ahead to Garden Plain to set up a roadblock, cohort Julius Finney and Adams wrecked on the bridge on the west side of Garden Plain. One was captured on the spot, and the other ran away, despite shouts to stop and several shots being fired his way. He was later found hiding under a bridge one mile north of town and captured, which resulted in a ten- to thirty-year sentence addition to his life sentence.

Once again, he engineered an escape, along with several other inmates who joined him, becoming the new Adams Gang. They robbed banks in Rose Hill and Haysville. Adams pistol-whipped an eighty-two-year-old man for no apparent reason, causing a skull fracture and his death. The police attempted to trap the gang near Anoly, Kansas, but they managed to escape, leaving Sheriff's Deputy Benjamin Fisher wounded.

The gang was spotted eleven days later after stealing $500 in silver from a bank in Osceola, Iowa. This led to an attempt to trap them near Murray, Iowa. A few miles from town, the gang rested on a gravel road, and a farmer named

C.J. Jones was suspicious and called Sheriff Ed West. A group was formed. As they approached the vehicle, a pistol was pointed point blank in the sheriff's face, but it failed to fire. He took cover, and a shootout ensued, with several members of the posse injured. Jones, hearing the gunfire, ran with his shotgun to assist, and the gang traded shots with him, leaving him mortally wounded.

The crime spree continued, with eleven stores in Muscotah, Kansas, being robbed. The gang also robbed two motorcycle officers outside Wichita and set their bikes on fire. On November 5, 1921, Adams shot and killed patrolman A.L. Young in cold blood. The gang's most successful heist was robbing a Santa Fe express train near Ottawa of $35,000. On the evening of November 20, Adams and several others were joy-riding around Wichita and were pulled over by two motorcycle policemen. A gunshot came from the vehicle, killing patrolman Robert Fitzpatrick. The car sped away, stranding in Cowley County two women who were just along for the ride. Later that night, the outlaws' car ran out of gas, and they attempted to steal a vehicle from farmer George Oldham. Oldham resisted, and Adams shot and killed him. Taking the stolen car back to Wichita, they went to the house of one of the men Adams was with; two police officers were waiting. Officer Ray Casner was shot and wounded, and Adams escaped.

On the day of Officer Fitzpatrick's funeral, Adams assumed that most of the police department would be there. He rented a car but was recognized. Three officers arrived, and Adams shot at them, fatally wounding Detective Charles Hoffman, who pulled him to the ground. Officer Charles Bowman was also wounded. D.C. Stuckey took cover behind a pillar and shot Adams three times, killing him.

Adams's body was put on display and was viewed by more than five thousand people. Even though this was the end of the era when bodies were put on public view, it was generally deemed necessary. Adams proved that there is no romanticism for killers.

NATURALIST CAMPS

One thing about Kansas is the fact that many march to the beat of a different drummer. From the early days with utopian societies and settlements to the naturalists of today, nothing quite stirs a community up like the thought of a nudist camp close by. Some have operated for years, and every so often there are many in the community who resist these camps.

One longtime camp is a former church camp near McLouth named Camp Gaea (Gaea means "Mother Earth"). Over the years, there has been controversy about the camp, which does not call itself a "nudist" camp but does have clothing-optional areas and considers itself a retreat area.

The camp caters to those of a different mindset, as well as to witches and pagan rituals. With all the hysteria, there have been many attempts to shut down these kinds of facilities through lawsuits and zoning. Though objectionable to many, there has been little success in using legal means to shut them down. Each facility has a variety of activities that go on throughout the year.

It has not been shown that anything illegal has occurred at the various camps, and there are several in operation around the state. With the exception of some drumming that may be heard late at night, there seems to be no impact on the surrounding communities. The existence of these camps just illustrates the variety of Kansans that exist. And in variety there is never boredom.

CARL S. ("STAN THE MAN") ENGDAHL

Growing up on a farm west of Marquette, Stan Engdahl loved to hunt, fish and trap. After he came home from the U.S. Army, he returned to Marquette and opened a radio and TV repair shop and started racing motorcycles. From 1946 to 1993, Stan became a five-time national motorcycle racing champion.

He was a charter member of the American Motorcycle Association, served on the city council for several terms, belonged to the American Legion and rose to be fire chief of McPherson Rural Fire District No. 2. Besides being a national champion racer, he was a sixteen-time Kansas state champion and won more than six hundred awards.

In 2003, in the radio and TV repair building, he put together the Kansas Motorcycle Museum. It was a natural thing to do because his collection was spreading through the building and into others. Stan and his wife were co-curators of the museum for many years. The museum at 120 North Washington in Marquette houses more than one hundred vintage motorcycles, photos, memorabilia, posters and more than six hundred trophies that Stan won in his racing career.

His other love was the fire department, and he served many years as fire chief. The McPherson County Rural Fire District No. 2 covers 219 square miles around Marquette. Stan spent many hours building trucks and equipment. On November 12, 2007, he went to the museum and had a good day visiting with people touring the collection. In the middle of the afternoon, he responded to a stove on fire in a house. As the fire was brought under control, he stepped out onto the porch and fell with a massive heart attack. Although the first responders started to work on him right away, he had passed.

As a tribute, the museum is still running with a group of volunteer enthusiasts and friends. Carl is on the National Fallen Firefighters Foundation Roll of Honor. He died at the age of seventy-eight.

THE RUNNYMEDE HOTEL

The Runnymede Hotel was built in 1889 at the English colony of Runnymede in Harper County, about twelve miles northeast of Harper. The colony of Runnymede was founded by an Irish promoter named Edward Turnly after his family purchased 1,700 acres of land. The colony was named after Runnymede, England, where in 1215 the Magna Carta was signed by King John, giving the citizens of England civil rights.

Turnly advertised that for $500 per year he would teach young gentlemen skills of farming and livestock raising at his "prairie paradise." The offer appealed to families of England, Ireland and Scotland who took the chance to send their young men overseas and amount to something.

In 1888, a general store was built and a post office opened. About one hundred men came, and businesses were started, joining the effort. There were groceries, dry goods, a creamery, livery stable, restaurants, a church and a stage line that went once a day to Harper and Norwich.

The boys sent over were fun-loving and irresponsible. They established courses and fields for horse racing, steeple chasing, polo, a bowling alley, a billiard parlor and tennis courts. By 1889, the town covered seven city blocks.

In 1889, the hotel was built—a magnificent showcase. It was three stories tall and offered all accommodations for the guests. It became the pride of the town. In 1891, there was a fire at the livery stable, and the hotel was nearly burned but ultimately was saved. Robert Watmough, a promoter and businessman of the town, was killed in the fire. Watmough's death was a blow to the spirits of the town and his friends.

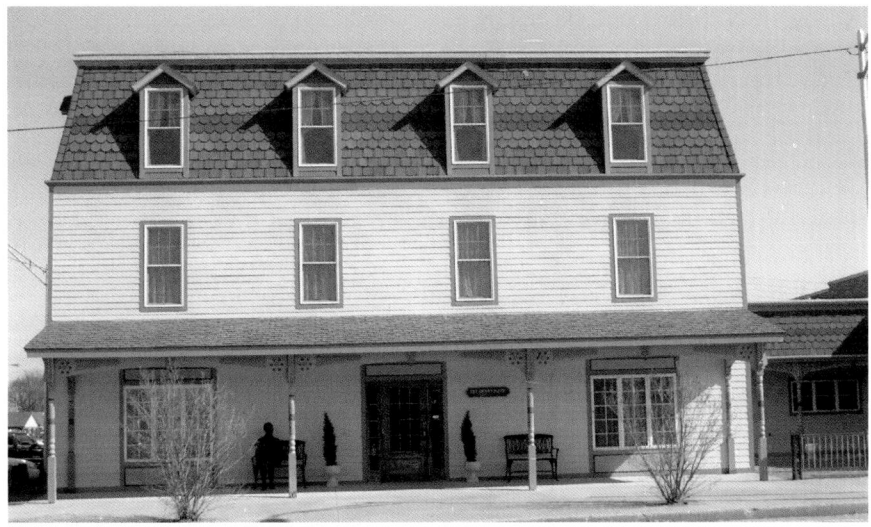

Runneymede Hotel in 2017 on town square, Alva, Oklahoma. *Photo by Roger Ringer.*

Relatives in England were alarmed at the news of the colony, and they were becoming tired of sending money. They became suspicious of the lifestyle and refused to send any more support. The demise of the colony was due to the loss of income, the Englishmen becoming bored and the country going into a depression. Also the Kansas, Mexico & Orient Railroad did not build track through the town but rather two miles away.

By 1892, the real estate was declared vacant due to nonpayment of taxes. Some buildings were moved to New Runnymede, which was at the tracks and the Harper Road. Three businessmen in Medicine Lodge bought the hotel in 1893. The opening of Oklahoma was two months away. The hotel was moved with horses and wagons, crossing four rivers and other streams before reaching its new home in Alva, Oklahoma.

The hotel went through several owners. It eventually became run-down and was close to being demolished. There was a cooperative effort to restore the hotel. Today, just off the Square in Alva, the fully restored Runnymede Hotel is operational as a venue and used for meetings, weddings, parties and other functions.

So, a piece of Kansas history is still alive, but in Oklahoma. One other piece of Runnymede is still available to view: the church. It was moved to Harper, and the Harper County Historical Society maintains it today. Just south of the Kingman/Harper County line on Highway K-2 is a roadside marker that tells the story of Runnymede.

RUDOLPH WENDELIN: SMOKEY THE BEAR

Rudolph Wendelin did not invent the Smokey the Bear image. There were at least ten prior artists that did the artwork for the U.S. Forest Service fire prevention icon. But he was the artist who gave Smokey his friendliness and personality. Starting with the U.S. Forest Service in 1933 as an illustrator and draftsman, Wendelin eventually worked full time on the Smokey the Bear Project.

Wendelin was born in Herndon up in Rawlins County. He studied architecture at the University of Kansas and studied art at several art schools. He served in the U.S. Navy through World War II and returned to the forest service in 1944. From 1944 until 1973, he was considered to be Smokey the Bear's caretaker. He completed hundreds of paintings of Smokey.

Wendelin also created many commemorative stamps, including a Forest Conservation stamp in 1958, Range Conservation stamp in 1961, John Muir stamp in 1964, John Wesley Powell stamp in 1969 and a Smokey the Bear stamp in 1984. In 1998, he received the Medal of Honor from the Daughters of the American Revolution for his work during the Smokey the Bear campaign. He was also awarded the Horace Hart Award from the graphic arts industry and both the Silver and Gold Smokey Bear Awards from the U.S. Department of Agriculture. Ironically, he designed the Smokey the Bear Awards one year before winning the first one.

Rudolph Wendelin was injured in a car accident on August 18, 2000. He died on August 31, 2000, as result of his injuries.

McLAIN'S ROUNDUP RODEO: SUN CITY

Marion F. "Mac" McLain started his famous roundup in Sun City in 1922. At the time, it was the largest privately owned rodeo in the country. The event ran from 1922 until 1939. The success of the rodeo is attributed to great planning and hard work. As big an event as it was in the rodeo world, and in the region of south-central Kansas and northern Oklahoma, it is not well known.

From the Barber County History Committee's *Chosen Land*:

> *"From the loudspeakers the stirring Sousa march, 'Stars & Stripes Forever,' blasts forth, all eyes focused on the arena gate as two mounted cowboys*

bearing the flags of the United States and the State of Kansas make their entrance. Next comes the rodeo owner and producer, M.F. 'Mac' McLain, flanked by his sons Max and Mark; they are followed by the contestants, clowns, trick riders, and Indians. Executing a specially designed marching pattern, they come to a halt and form a line in the middle of the arena. The spirited horses paw the turf and chomp at their bits as the band strikes up The National Anthem. The applause is thunderous and matched by the honking of cars parked in their stalls. Then whoop and holler, they charge out the exit gates to get ready for the first event."

Such was the spectacular grand entrée which sets the stage for the Annual McLain Roundup which was not only in the history of Sun City and Barber County, but in the State of Kansas. The success of the rodeo was due to much planning and work. Days before the event, an advertising caravan of cars drove thru surrounding towns making residents "rarin to go." That Mac was a master showman was evident the moment one crossed the bridge south of town and turned left. The trunk of every tree along the lane was white washed, as were the corral fences and barns. White teepees of the Cheyenne Indians were erected at the western edge of the grounds. Led by Chief Morris Medicine, they were to perform during the rodeo. On the eve of the celebrations sightseers were invited to witness tribal rituals and dances. A steer was butchered and cut into strips to dry on poles for their use during the three day affair.

The rodeo began at 1:30 p.m. and provided a full afternoon's program. Events were as follows: bronc and steer riding, wild cow milking, calf roping, buffalo and cattelo riding, circling riding, relay races, three horse races, Roman and chariot races and chuck wagon races. Each year, the event became bigger and better, as advertised.

The contest drew many from near and far since anyone could participate, provided they had an entry fee. World champion contestants vying for purses were Bob Crosby, Irby Mundy, Everett Shaw, Ike Rude and Bud Hampton, to name a few, as well as local cowboys. Rodeo clowns like Pinky Gist and Charlie Shultz not only entertained the crowds with their antics but also plied their trade, expertly risking life and limb. Recording the rodeo on film was Homer Venters, veteran cameraman. Oftentimes his Graphex was tossed over the fence ahead of him as he scrambled out of the way of many a raging animal.

It has been many years since the song especially written for the roundup, "Rarin to Go," has been heard in the Medicine River Valley. There has been

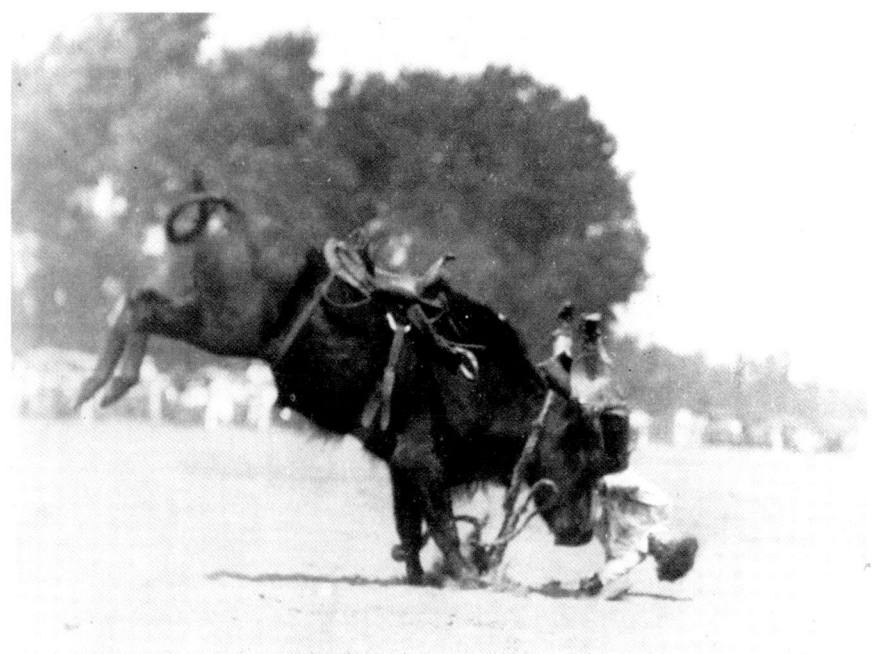

Bucking off a buffalo, McLain Rodeo, Sun City. *Courtesy of Brenda McLain, photo by Homer Venters.*

thought of reviving the roundup, but it takes an imaginative person with driving ambition to re-create something of this magnitude in a community of 72 people and a county of 4,500, especially when the same communities create the Medicine Lodge Peace Treaty Pageant every few years.

Mac has been nominated for membership in the Western Heritage Cowboy Hall of Fame Museum. The hope is someday that the song "Rarin to Go" will be heard at an induction ceremony.

ORVILLE BROWN: WORLD CHAMPION WRESTLER

Orville Brown was born at Sharon, Kansas, on March 10, 1908. He grew up on a farm and walked to Kiowa several miles to go to school. He only was able to attend his freshman year of high school and quit to work. He was orphaned at age eleven and worked on farms in the area.

Like most boys, he was up early milking cows and lived with relatives. He worked the fields and took care of livestock. He became a helper for a local blacksmith.

He became a farm and ranch hand and went on to become a professional rodeo cowboy. When he heard of a good rodeo, he would go and put his money down. By the time he was eighteen, he had become one of the top rodeo hands in the business. He excelled in bulldogging, bareback and saddle bronc riding. He bulldogged a steer in 4.8 seconds. In an exhibition at the Briggs Ranch, he was the first to bulldog a buffalo from horseback.

He had a job in 1926 at Leonardville, where he eloped with a farmer's daughter, Grace, a marriage that lasted nearly fifty-five years. He continued as a rodeo cowboy when the country went into a depression, and he had to shuck corn to make ends meet. Becoming too heavy to compete anymore in the rodeo, he was working full time on a farm, with Grace working for the farmer also. This was near Wallace. He found that a blacksmith was needed in town. He soon became accomplished at this.

Being naturally strong, the work of a blacksmith hardened him and made him stronger. A man came in one day and was watching Orville work when he asked him, "With a body like that, what are you doing in this little town?" The man had experience as a promoter of amateur wrestling and agreed to work out with him and teach him. The local high school let them use a mat, and the high school boys worked out with him. He started working matches around western Kansas. A promoter set Orville up with a professional, intending to end his career, but to their surprise, Orville went on to seventy-two wins in a row.

A top promoter in the country got wind of him and sent him to St. Louis. The promoter advised him to go back east and start wrestling good athletes. With Orville not knowing how he would afford to get back home, the promoter pulled out his checkbook and wrote a check for $5,000. In Depression money, he never thought he could pay him back.

He soon shot up the ranks and was in contention for a world championship. He competed at Madison Square Garden and beat some of the best wrestlers of his time. He had a grueling match with the world champion, Jim Landos, and had him beaten on the mat when Orville tried a third tackle to finish him. When he flew through the ropes onto the concrete outside the mat, the referee was forced to count him out and Landos the winner, even when he was lying passed out on the mat. Orville was given a rematch with Landos that ended in a draw. In the third match, a wrong decision by the referee cost

Orville the win. Before another match could be rescheduled, Landos had sailed for Dublin to meet Danno O'Mahoney. Not realizing he had three broken ribs, Landos lost to the Irishman and retired.

In 1937, Orville wrestled in the first televised match in history. No one saw it outside the hotel since there was no transmission, but it set the stage for the future of televised wrestling. In Columbus, Ohio, on June 28, 1940, he finally became the undisputed champion of the world, winning the Diamond Belt. Orville was the catalyst to form the National Wrestling Alliance, which was a truly national organization.

Then, disaster struck. Orville had hired Bobby Burns to be a sparring partner in preparation for a major match with Lou Thesz. They were topping a hill near Bethany, Missouri, when a semitrailer crossed the road. They went under the trailer and became lodged there. Both Orville and Bobby were nearly decapitated. He lay in the hospital unconscious for days. When he came to, they discovered he had paralysis on his right side.

He regained his health but not his quickness and had to quit the ring. He became a promoter and retired from wrestling altogether in 1957. It hurt him to see how television and unscrupulous people ruined wrestling. Many would compare the great wrestlers of the day and since, and Orville Brown is considered one of the best.

Orville Brown—the orphan, cowboy, blacksmith and world champion wrestler from Sharon, Kansas—died in 1981 at Marysville, Missouri. Following in his father's footsteps, Orville and Grace's son became a professional wrestler as well.

TOAD PLAGUE

McPherson was especially hard hit from time to time with toad plagues. The other surrounding towns and rural areas would be assumed to have the same problems. The McPherson Wetlands, five miles west of McPherson, would pose this challenge to everyday living in drier years. The wetlands were full of toads and tadpoles. It was noted that as the conditions dried up, the movement of toads began to take place.

Following is the text of a newspaper story that was printed in the *McPherson Daily Tribune* on Saturday June 29, 1901. This was picked up by the *Los Angeles Herald* and other newspapers across the country:

> MCPHERSON, KANSAS: This city has suffered from a toad plague. The recent dry weather has caused the bogs and swamps which surround McPherson to dry up and the toads, which are unusually numerous this year, have invaded the town. Traffic of all kinds has been suspended. Street cars, bicycles, and buggies can hardly be driven along the streets for fear of the toads. City officials will take steps to rid the town of the pest.

According to many accounts, it was not possible to walk after dark without stepping on a toad with every step. There are no notes on how long the plague of toads lasted, but it would be safe to assume that it was for very long periods of time. There is also no mention of how city officials ever remedied the plague of toads.

It is noted that driving while the toads covered the roadways was not easily accomplished. Such events furnished material for biblical plagues for Sunday sermons. It may also have lessened the opposition to the draining of the wetlands when the idea came to fruition.

LAST EXECUTION IN SEDGWICK COUNTY JAIL

The last execution that took place at the Sedgwick County Jail was on November 21, 1888. What was unusual about this execution was that the crime had not taken place in Sedgwick County but rather in Indian Territory. Being that the case was brought before federal court in Wichita, the prisoners were held at the Sedgwick County Jail and thus the eventual execution was also held there.

The men who were convicted of first-degree murder and executed for the crime were brothers. Jake and Joe Tobler, listed in most accounts as "colored," had been convicted of murdering Frank Cass and A.P. "Goody" Kountz, two merchants on their way from Texas to Vinita, Indian Territory. The two merchants stopped to camp under a tree one mile from the Sac & Fox Agency on August 16, 1885. The Tobler brothers were camped nearby and at a late hour crept up on the sleeping figures and shot them.

The brothers proceeded to steal the merchants' wagon and team of horses and stripped the bodies of four dollars, a gold watch and a ring before they drove to their uncle's home. The bodies were found and identified by a brother of one of the victims, and then a "half breed" came forward and said that he had heard the shots and saw the two murderers ride off.

A posse of seven men took up the trail of the murderers, and on August 19, 1885, the Toblers were arrested for the murders. Both prisoners immediately confessed to the men of the posse, and the two were taken to await action by a grand jury in Wichita. Both men were indicted, and Jake's trial began on September 5, 1885. There was considerable argument from the defense to exclude the confession of guilt to the posse, as well as testimony of the witness. Jake's possession of the stolen property when arrested sealed his fate. The jury only took fifteen minutes to bring back a conviction for first-degree murder.

Joe's trial was the next day and had the same results, only the jury came back with a guilty verdict in seven minutes. Appeals, applications and executive clemency delayed the executions for several years. Finally, the brothers were sentenced to hang. Both men had been held in the old jail but were transferred to the new jail. They shared cells with a man named Thurber and a man named Fraizer. Both men were model prisoners and never gave jailer Ed Darnell any trouble.

On the night before the execution, the scaffold was tested at 10:00 p.m. and worked perfectly. The execution was scheduled for between 9:00 a.m. and noon. Even before the appointed times, those witnesses with proper credentials assembled at the jail. The crowd of eighty-four consisted of deputy marshals, doctors in the interest of science, newspaper representatives and Reverend Gates of the First Methodist Episcopal Church, assisted by Mr. and Mrs. Cole and Mr. Harper, a ministerial student.

The prisoners spent a nervous night. They played cards, ate peanuts and drank spirits. Shortly after 9:00 a.m., Mr. and Mrs. Cole and Mr. Harper gained admittance to the prisoners' cell, where they sang hymns and offered prayers. The prisoners were joking as to whether their bravery would last or if they would make fools of themselves. They lit cigars, walked nervously around their cells and called for stimulants. They were asked if they would want to see other prisoners and say goodbye. They said yes and, in the charge of Sheriff Hays, passed by the other cells, met with ready hands and asked, "How are you?"

In charge of the proceedings was Charles Howard of Topeka and Joe McClellan, sheriff of Kingman County. Others present were W.A. Jarrett of Caldwell, Jack Stilwell of the Indian Territory and Deputies H. Metcalf and Henry Dillard of Topeka. At 10:18 a.m., Deputy Howard beckoned for the jailer to open the door, leading the condemned men to the hall. Deputy

Howard read the death warrant. At 10:25 a.m., the lever was pulled; the drop was four and a half feet. Jake never moved, dead from a broken neck. Joe moved after fifty seconds and drew his shoulders slightly forward, and during the second minute, he drew up his legs twice. At the end of the sixth minute, both were pronounced dead by County Physician Rentz. They were allowed to hang for fifteen minutes and then put into coffins and taken to a local parlor, where hundreds viewed the remains.

EMMA CHASE: SUE SMITH

Cottonwood Falls is a historic town that has embraced its history and has gotten recognition from all over the state, nation and even the world. The historic Chase County Courthouse is the crown jewel overlooking the main business district of town. But what had gotten the most attention for the town for many years was the Emma Chase Café.

Emma Chase is a fictional character, but not from a play or some romance novel, even though you can find an actual author of romance novels named Emma Chase. The character was created by two women who took the old five and dime building and opened a café. Linda Thurston and Linda Woody opened the restaurant (ownership of the building had been secured in the 1980s by local residents hoping that a café would open there). In searching for a name, they chose "Emma" because it sounded vaguely historical and "Chase" because of the name of the county where it was located.

Then came Sue, who was raised in Cottonwood Falls. Sue had trained as a nurse and moved to Texas, where she met and married a rancher named Monty Smith. They moved to Cottonwood Falls when Sue became director of nurses at the local nursing home. So, what does one do when retiring? Like many people who have the entrepreneurial spirit and a sense of history, she started a new life. In 1998, she leased the Emma Chase Café.

Featuring down-home cooking, the Emma Chase Café was on the grow. When the building next door became available, Sue and Monty acquired it and opened a shop with antiques, jams and jellies, rustic cookware and books. Also, Sue brought Emma Chase to life by playing the part of the fictional character.

And then came the music, though quite by accident. Someone mentioned to her one day that "for fifty cents he would hang a note over at the barbershop to see if anyone was interested in 'jamming.'" Twelve musicians showed up the first time, followed by twenty-five family members. Eventually, they had to move the jam to the street, and it became a tradition. Down the street, there was an old municipal building that had been many things, including a skating rink. When the weather is not right, they meet there. Now it is a cooperative of Flint Hills artists and antiques.

When things come to an end, there is often a little panic. Sue decided one day that it was time to retire once again. A new group has the Emma Chase (or Prairie Past Times), and the music and art goes on. New people plan on running a new restaurant in the old Emma Chase Café. New businesses still operate on Main Street in Cottonwood Falls. There is even a song about the Emma Chase by an Australian artist who attends the Walnut Valley Festival at Winfield and has become good friends of Sue and Monty's.

Sue has been involved with many things, including the Statewide Ball, the Prairie Fire Festival, the Flint Hills Folk Life Festival and the Broom Weed Festival. When asked what she would do after retiring from the café, she replied, "Honey, I was retired when I started this."

KANSANS INVENT BULLDOZER

When you say the word *bulldozer*, the image that you envision is the classic Caterpillar bulldozer, which has become the standard for heavy earth moving and other operations that require big pushing and pulling power and a light weight load in soft situations. Today's designs come from the Best and Holt traction engines, which were known at the time as "track layers." The merging of the two companies created the Caterpillar Company, which is the leader in bulldozers today.

But the original concept of a bulldozer was invented in Kansas—to be specific, in Morrowville, Kansas. James Cummings was a young farmer in Washington County, and he was watching the Sinclair Oil Company laying a pipeline through the area. The pipeline was being run from the Teapot Dome area of Wyoming to refineries in Freeman, Missouri. The actual digging process had been mechanized, but backfilling the trench was still old school, done with mules and dirt slips. It was a time-consuming and expensive process. He knew there had to be a better way to do it. Typical of the Kansas farm boy problem-solving and mechanical knowhow, he dreamed up a design.

With the help of a local draftsman, J. Earl McLeod, Cummings's designs were put on paper. He approached the oil company about the idea of pushing the dirt in mechanically, and it encouraged him to bring in something. Taking from the iron piles and using parts of a Model T frame, windmill springs and other materials, Cummings and McLeod built the first bulldozer.

The trial was so successful that the men were awarded a contract to backfill the pipeline from Deshler, Nebraska, to Freeman, Missouri. The concept was very elementary, and the pair collaborated on other inventions. The partnership ended with the death of McLeod's wife, as McLeod then sold his partnership and went back to Washington County.

The first bulldozer was pretty rudimentary and was actually a wooden blade mounted on a farm tractor, the first one being a Fordson. The original bulldozer does not exist today, but a replica of it is on display in the city park at Morrowville. The bulldozer is a pretty crude machine, but it started off the technology. The success of the design when applied to a crawler tractor has proven the most efficient way to utilize the original concept.

Although the design was patented, it is not known how much value actually reached the inventor. Cummings did much more design and work

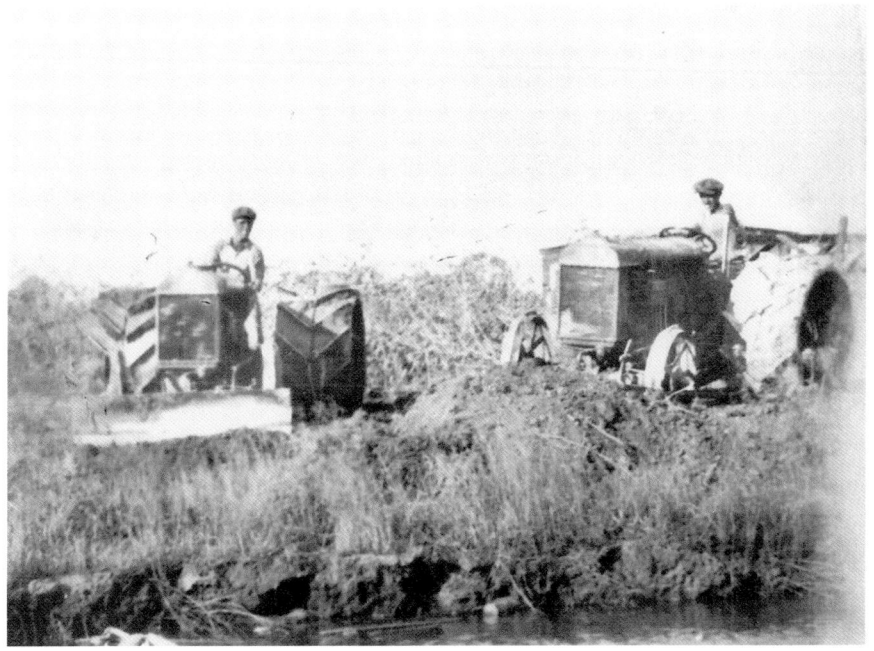

First bulldozer working on pipeline. *Courtesy of Duane Durst.*

in the oil fields over the years. His designs have been credited with helping to win World War II. The bulldozer gave workers the ability to accomplish more work in a day than was thought possible. His other inventions include the side winch and boom, a pipe-wrapping machine, a cold pipe bender, a thermostatically controlled tar kettle and a mechanism to apply weighted material to a pipe in water jobs. He went on to work pipeline jobs all over the world.

James became a lifetime counselor at Texas Agricultural and Mechanical College (Texas A&M). He was recognized by the National and International Pipeline Contractors Association with a life membership. He received the Presidential E (Excellence) Award from the U.S. Department of Defense on October 12, 1964.

James lived in Texas for the rest of his life and was very generous in supporting local causes such as 4-H, the Hays County Hospital and the Hays County Youth Association, and he owned Green Valley Livestock Auction. Cummings died on May 27, 1981.

A Cummings bulldozer replica is in the park at Morrowville and can be seen anytime. It is enclosed in a fence under a roof.

JIM FARRELL

Many musicians end up going to Nashville, but Tennessee Jim Farrell did it just the opposite way. He was born in, grew up in and moved from Nashville to Kansas. Jim grew up with harmony and music. His father was a choral director and was in a barbershop quartet. His mother sang in the Nashville Symphony Chorale. Growing up, Jim and his sister, Stephanie, were expected to join in on cue with harmony as they drove down the highway. By the age of fourteen, he was an accomplished musician, playing bass professionally with adult groups. By age sixteen, he was backing artists who performed at the Grand Ole Opry. Over the next few years, he learned many instruments, including keyboard, guitar, bass and percussion.

Growing up, his best friend was Ben Hall of Home Place Studios, and he worked off and on with Ben for twenty years. Ben had traveled as a fellow performer with Elvis. In the early years, Ben had recorded with many music icons, such as Buddy Holly and the Crickets, Roy Orbison and Alabama. Jim was groomed to be a session musician, producer and music publisher. He also helped Ben build two different recording studios where Ben taught him to hear acoustics, sound frequencies, pick his songs, co-write music and be a contributing member of the music industry in Nashville. Jim has played on hundreds of studio sessions, meeting musical greats from Jeannie C. Riley to Garth Brooks.

Jim studied music on a full scholarship at David Lipscomb College in Nashville and was one of the first students in recording industry management at Middle Tennessee State University. Later, he excelled in video production at Davidson School of Business.

Jim always loved the close harmonies of western music. Jim met Stu Stuart in Nashville in the 1990s. They formed the group J-38 Land and Cattle Company with lawman Clay Jerrolds. A few years after Clay's death, Stu returned home to Kansas. He recruited Jim to come to Kansas and form a new group, the Prairie Rose Wranglers. Over the next eight years, the group helped build the Prairie Rose Chuckwagon Supper near Benton, Kansas, which became a major tourist attraction. The group went on major

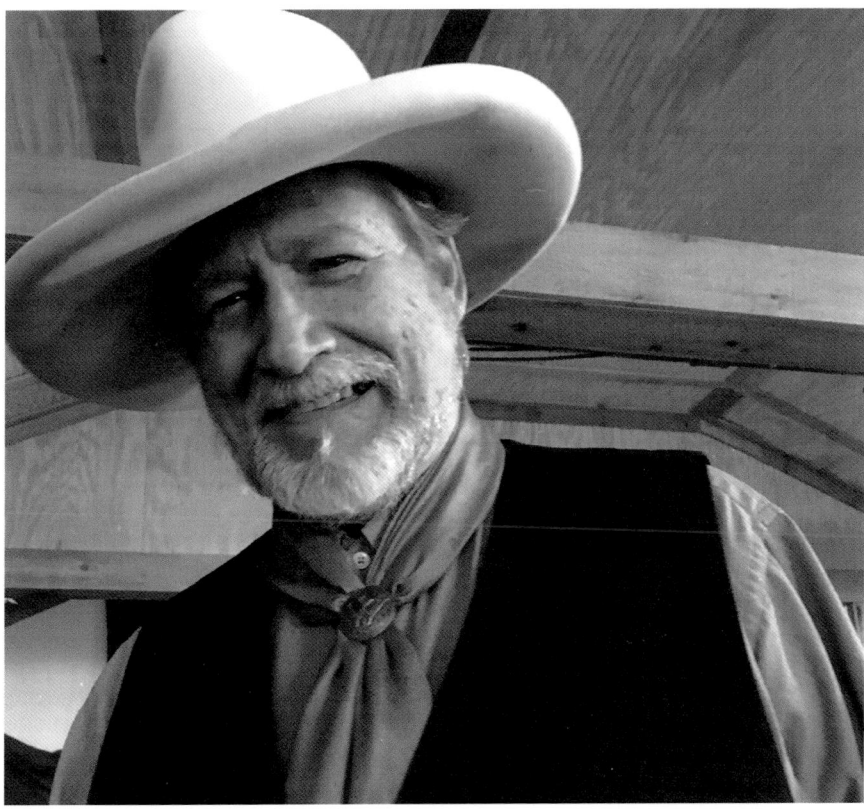

Jim Farrell. *Courtesy of Jim Farrell Studios.*

tours along with several other western artists from Carnegie Hall to the Great Wall of China. It still has the first permit ever issued for a concert on the Great Wall of China.

In 2007, the group changed its name to the Diamond W Wranglers and moved its home base to Old Cowtown Museum in Wichita. Jim has written scores for symphony so the band can offer a unique experience backed by an orchestra. It has recorded many albums over the years and is popular all over the Midwest.

In a small, nondescript building in Towanda, Kansas, Jim has built the Jim Farrell Studios. Jim has recorded and produced albums for many artists, including Rex Allen Jr. and Roy Rogers Jr.; he has also traveled with both artists. Jim won Western Album Producer of the Year from the Hall of Great Western Performers, Cowboy Hall of Fame. Jim and his group have won awards for excellence from the Western Music Association and the Academy of Western Artists.

Jim was fortunate to meet and marry Martha Slater Farrell, who owns First Generation Video. They now combine their talents and businesses and collaborate on projects from their studio in Towanda.

Jim has become an officer and board member of the Kansas Chapter of the Western Music Association, which Ray Amerine and Johnny Western cofounded. The production "Kansas: Home on the Range" was performed at the Historic Fox Theatre in Hutchinson, Kansas, in 2011 to celebrate Kansas's 150th birthday and again at the official celebration of the Kansas 150 at Century II Auditorium in Wichita. Jim and Martha were a key part of the production.

BUFFALO JONES: CHARLES JESSE JONES

In a picture there are three westerners posing together: William F. "Buffalo Bill" Cody, Charles J. "Buffalo" Jones and Gordon "Pawnee Bill" Lillie. Most have heard of the two showmen, but Buffalo Jones has been lost to the mist of history. Yet he is probably the one who achieved the most in the real building of the West than the other two who portrayed the West.

Much of Buffalo Jones's work was done in Kansas, but he went on to be so important that he is credited with saving the American bison from extinction and is a resident in a few halls of fame. Many would know him as a builder of Garden City. He was one of the founding fathers there. He convinced the

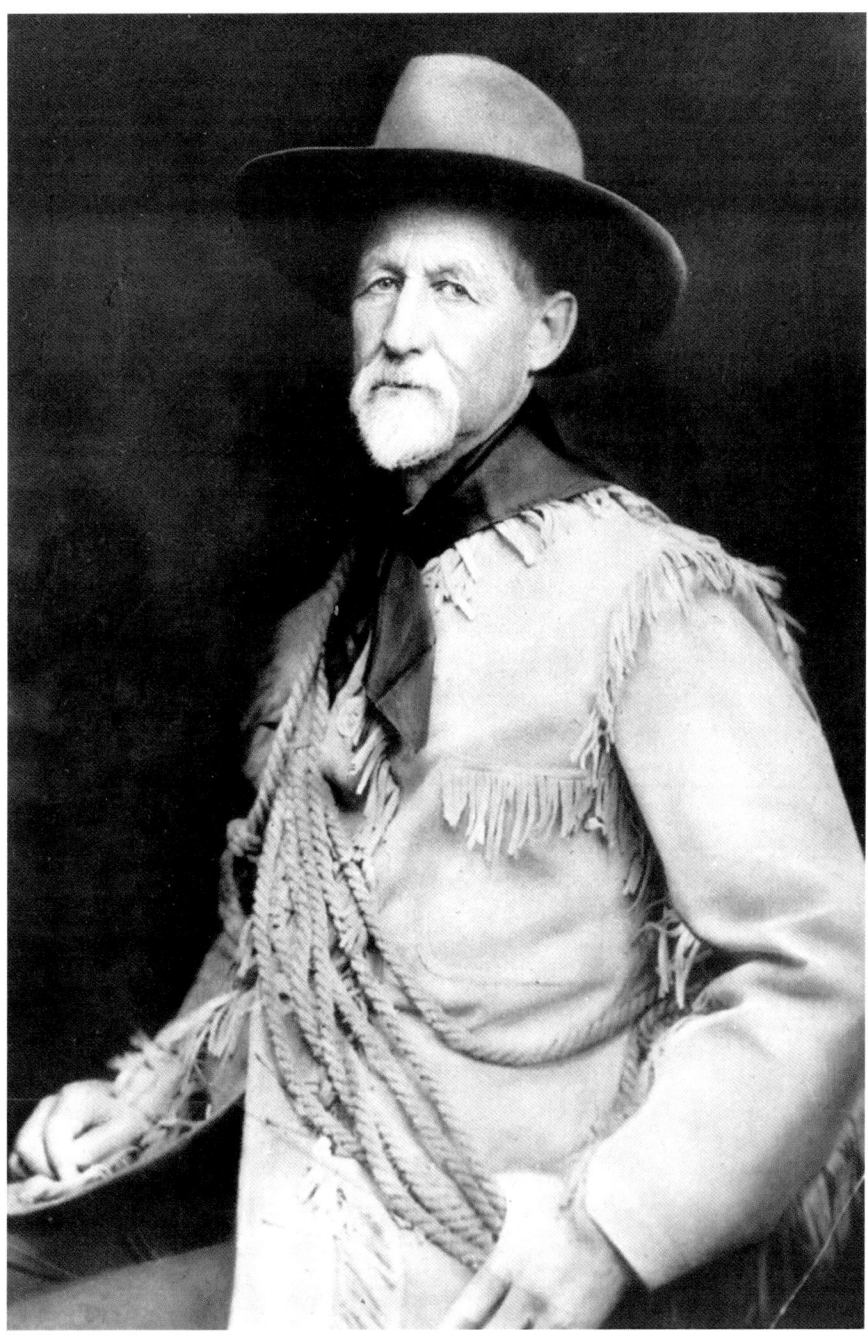

Charles Jesse Jones, aka Buffalo Jones. *Courtesy of Finney County Historical Museum.*

railroad to put a stop and siding there and then built a depot. But let's go back to the beginning.

Charles Jesse Jones was the third of twelve children born in Money Township, McLean County, Illinois, to Noah and Jane (Munden) Jones. Abraham Lincoln was a family friend and a frequent visitor on the family farm. At age seventeen, Charles entered Illinois Wesleyan University, but typhoid fever made him give up his studies. So he went west and came to Troy, Kansas, in 1866. Jones married Martha J. Walton and had six children. He built a stone house and started a nursery. While living in Troy, he ventured out west to hunt buffalo. He was intrigued by the hairy beasts and the fact that money could be made from selling the hides. He moved the family to Osborne County on January 1, 1872, to be closer to the range.

Jones had planned to go to the Sandwich Islands to recover a buried treasure that was marked on a map he had come into possession of, but that dream was never realized. In 1874, Jones was appointed undersheriff of Osborn County. Being away so often on hunting trips, he learned the art of scouting and plainsmanship. There are some reports that he arrived at the nickname "Buffalo" to differentiate him from "Dirty Faced" Jones and "Wrong Wheel" Jones, characters of that time. More likely it was because of his turning from shooting buffalo to saving them.

In 1876, Jones moved to Sterling. Three years later, he became a founding father, with three others, of the city of Garden City. He was also called Colonel Jones by some. In 1885, Jones completed the stone courthouse and presented it, with surrounding lots, to the county as a gift. Jones was also the first representative from Finney County in the Kansas legislature. By 1886, he had realized that the buffalo would soon be killed off completely and began to collect buffalo on his ranch. He made trips to the Texas Panhandle and roped and brought back several buffalo calves. He assembled a herd of more than 150 animals. The other remaining herd was in Yellowstone, and the two herds were eventually merged. Many buffalo today descend from that herd. He had also started another ranch near McCook, Nebraska, for his buffalo.

In 1891, he took ten full-grown animals to London and gave them to the Zoological Gardens there; he also presented the Prince of Wales with a buffalo robe. This did strain his finances, and he returned to Troy for a while. In 1893, he made the Cherokee Strip land run and took a claim near Perry, Oklahoma. He was also working on the coast promoting a railroad. He found national attention when he took a trip to the Arctic to rope musk ox. This trip did not succeed, but he spent a little time in the Alaska Gold Rush.

Returning to Troy in 1898, he penned his autobiography, *Buffalo Jones: 40 Years of Adventure*. The book came out in 1899, and in July 1902, President Theodore Roosevelt appointed him as the first game warden of Yellowstone National Park. He held that position until 1905, when he resigned over a dispute with the army, which administered the park. Jones also experimented several times, trying to develop the cattalo, which is a cross of a bison and a cow. He then established a ranch on the rim of the Grand Canyon. A dentist from New York City visited Jones, hoping to improve his health. Together, Jones and Zane Grey roped and relocated mountain lions, and Grey wrote his first book, *The Last of the Plainsmen*, with Jones as the hero. The movie *Buffalo Rider* fictionalized Jones's life.

In 1910, Jones made a trip to Africa to rope live animals and lectured around the country about his adventures. A second trip to Africa to rope gorillas failed; he contracted jungle fever and suffered a heart attack. He never recovered, dying on October 2, 1919. He is buried at Valley View Cemetery in Garden City. He is honored in the National Buffalo Association Hall of Fame, the Osborne County Hall of Fame and the Hall of Great Western Performers, Cowboy Hall of Fame.

WANTHA DAVIS: JOCKEY

Born Wantha Bangs in Liberal on January 3, 1917, Wantha Davis-Bangs is considered the greatest female jockey of all time in horse racing, winning one thousand races. In 1931, she started galloping horses in the Liberal area. Wantha graduated from high school at Liberal in 1934. From 1934 until 1939, she rode horses in races in Dodge City and Winfield in Kansas, Hartnew and Seiling in Oklahoma and across the western United States, including New Mexico and California.

In 1939, she married Lendol Davis. She rode relay in the Cheyenne Frontier Days Rodeo, won the New Mexico State Fair with her own mount and galloped horses in Washington State. She galloped horses at Churchill Downs but was never allowed to race there. The Civil Rights Act eventually forced Churchill Downs to open for female jockeys, but the change of rules came twelve years after she retired.

Wantha was the first sanctioned female rider to ride pari-mutuel races. She raced at Lincoln, Hastings and Columbus in Nebraska. She galloped horses at all major tracks but was always turned down to get her jockey license. She ran a race in Mexico against Hall of Famer Johnny Longden, winning by a length and three quarters. The three-time national champion was so mad he refused to weigh out. People crossed the border from San Diego to Aguascalientes, Mexico, to watch the race. She also beat Hall of Famers Glen Lasswell and Basil James. She won roughly half of all races she was in.

Wantha rode for top trainers, owners and breeders such as Marion van Berg, Walter Merrick and Rex Ellsworth. She competed on equal footing with all top jockeys in the sport and beat most of them. She always said that she was never scared: "When you are on a horse, you don't have time to think about your nerves." She always preferred to coax her horses by hand rather than use the whip; she always knew the right words to use for each horse.

Since there were no facilities at racetracks for female jockeys, she made her horse trailer into a portable dressing room. She rode the circuit of western dirt half-mile tracks. Without a license, she had to ride wherever able. She commented, "I rode in places so wild and wooly; there were steers and bucking horses." (In the early days, they rode steers and not bulls.)

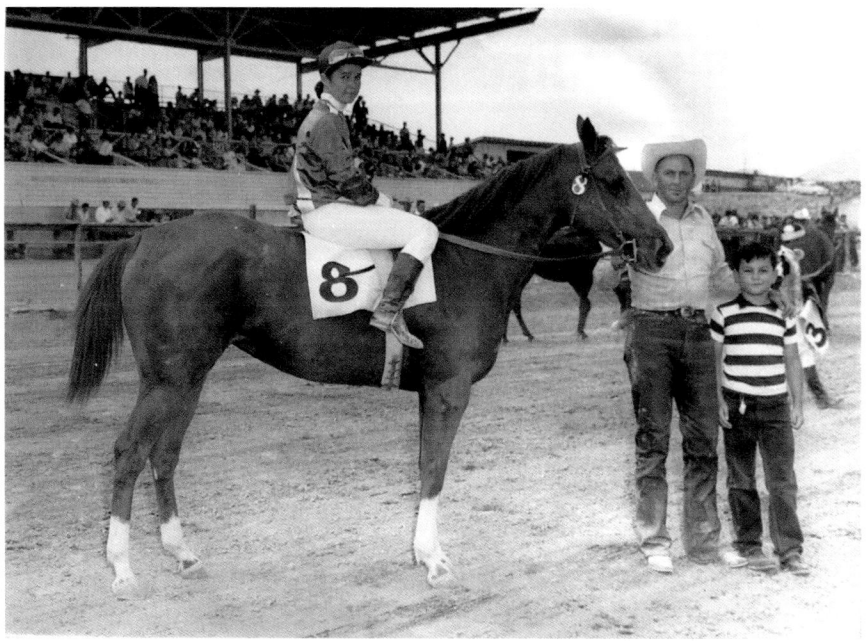

Wantha Davis. *Courtesy of Tad Davis.*

Wantha grew up one mile from a track at Liberal, and it was just natural for her to ride at an early age. As a small girl, she had her own Shetland pony named Merrylegs, a gift from her grandfather. As soon as her legs could reach the stirrups, a neighbor let her ride a black mare. She entered her first race at age fifteen. After finishing high school, she rode a freight train to Texas with fifty cents in her pocket. Within a day, she had found work as an "exercise boy." She galloped horses in the early mornings before races.

Lendol Davis, whom she married, was a horse breeder and racetrack regular. They had one son, Tad, and they would tour the race circuits with a trailer. The car contained all possessions and pets, and they would sleep on the side of the road when there was no money for a motel.

After retiring, the couple bought an 850-acre ranch near Duncan, Oklahoma. After Lendol died, Wantha continued to operate the ranch. When Wantha retired, she moved to Austin, Texas, to be near her grandchildren and serve as an inspiration. She said, "Hard work, with respect, discipline, and cleanliness for body, mind, and soul is my recipe for being a winner."

In 2004, Wantha was inducted into the Cowgirl Hall of Fame. As of this writing, she has been nominated for the Thoroughbred Hall of Fame and the Quarter Horse Hall of Fame. She was always soft-spoken and modest about her victories over male jockeys. When she died on September 18, 2012, it was only with the discovery of a box full of her newspaper clippings that the family knew what a pioneer and champion she had been.

MARGARET ANN McKENZIE: WICHITA CARRIAGE WORKS

At a time when women were just starting to rally around voting rights, personal rights and freedom, there was a woman overlooked in the history of Kansas. In Wichita, the outstanding woman in the formation of the city was the one woman who signed the original charter for the establishment of Wichita as a city, Catherine McCarty, more famously known as the mother of Billy the Kid.

After the city was established, a couple came to town and opened a factory in 1884, building carriages, wagons and fire equipment. Margaret Ann (Friend) McKenzie came with her husband, Daniel McKenzie, and established the Wichita Carriage Works. Working together to expand the business, they were soon joined by several competitors in the community.

The attention to detail and fine workmanship allowed the company to grow and build a reputation.

Margaret Ann Friend was born in London, Ontario, Canada. She married Daniel F. McKenzie, who was born in Michigan and whose mother was from London, Ontario. Coming to Wichita in 1884, they established the Wichita Carriage Works. As the business was booming and employed many men in the company, Daniel had a paralyzing stroke and was an invalid for seventeen years. Although Daniel was no longer able to run the company, Margaret kept the business running for seventeen years until Daniel's death and then continued on after that. Her two sons, Leo and Donald, grew up literally in the business. Reportedly, son Leo sold his first carriage to the Innes family at age twelve.

Margaret ran all aspects of the company and was admired as one of the best business people in the country. This fact was reported in the magazine *Blacksmith & Wheelwright* in its January 1916 issue. The company was renamed the M.A. McKenzie Body Works and continued to survive through the ups and downs of the economy and the end of the horse as primary transportation. The transition through rubber tires on the automobile was negotiated by the company under Margaret's steady hand and clear vision.

The elite of the region were strong customers of the carriages and phaetons, which were stylish and of superior quality. The first paddy wagon for the Wichita Police Department was built by the company. The first two hose wagons built for the fire department and several fire chiefs' buggies were built by the company as well.

The second factory was called a wonder by the local press. The new two-story brick-over-frame factory was built next to the old factory. For many years, there were about twenty-eight employees on average through all the ups and downs. When the transition to the automobile and trucks was accomplished, the company employed about two hundred men on average.

As Margaret aged and started to turn over more responsibilities to her two sons, she still came in every day and oversaw the company. It is a wonder that the impact of Margaret on the standing of competence in business and life has not caught the attention of those who look to heroes to use as an example of how a woman can do the job that a man can do, even in a time when this was almost unknown.

As the company grew and diversified, it was noticed that bus bodies, and other specialty applications for commercial vehicles, carried the M.A. McKenzie Body Works tag and, later, Leo McKenzie Body Works. After

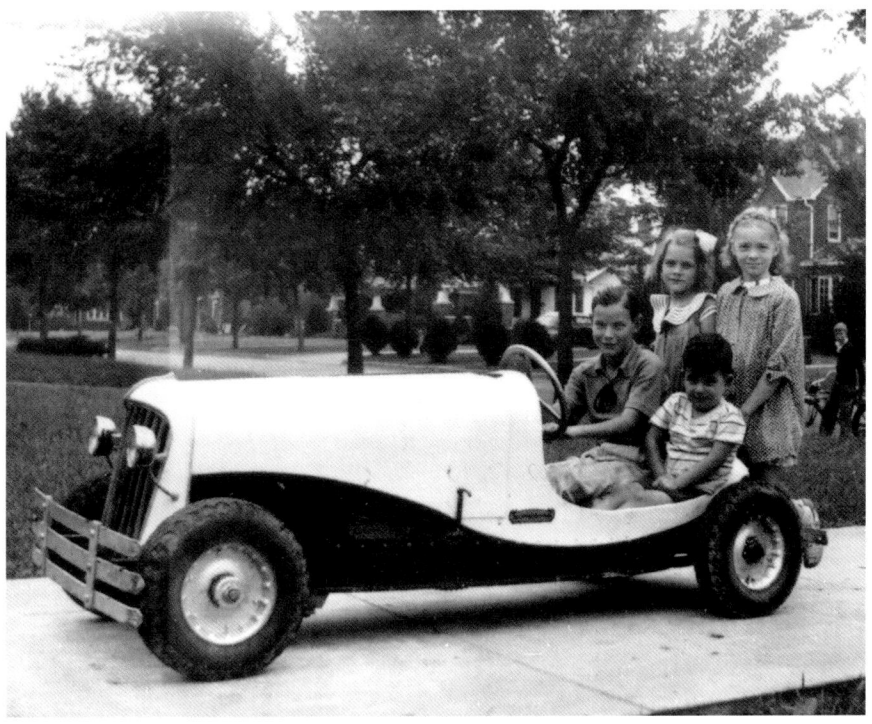

McKenzie miniature automobile. *Courtesy of Wichita-Sedgwick County Historical Museum.*

Margaret's death, there was a court action between sons Leo and Donald about ownership of the company. Leo went on to work at the original company, but there is not much on record about Donald. But that is another story.

SYDIA WIRT SPRECKLES: KANSAS TURKISH PRINCESS

Sidi, as she was called, was born to a successful western Kansas and eastern Colorado father who was a pioneer in the ranching business, one of the founders of Garden City and one of the largest businessmen of the area. Born Sydia, the newspapers used various spellings of her name over the years, from "Sydia" to "Sidi," "Ciddie" and other variations. Her father was E.L. (Edward) Wirt. He came to the area in 1871 when he was fifteen years old. The region was populated by Indians, buffalo and cattle. He spent many years on the range and spent a great deal of time working for the Holly & Sullivan Ranch, living for a time in the Holly, Colorado area. He was married to Miss Clara Fulton, the daughter of pioneer and Garden City founder W.D. Fulton. After living in Holly, Colorado, for one year, they moved to the new town of Garden City. Being involved in the stock growing business, Ed was also a progressive farmer and businessman. Ed was instrumental in developing the sugar beet industry.

Sidi was one of three daughters born to Ed and Clara. Sidi was the apple of her father's eye, and he was amused at the shenanigans she became involved in, like sliding down the main stair banister in the hotel in town. She was very talented and attended the University of Kansas. She also went to Valparaiso University Conservatory of Music. The timeline becomes confused, as Sidi performed in both the Chicago area and in New York. In 1910, she announced her engagement to Hugo Leal, who was a wealthy Brazilian count and businessman. However, at the same time, Sidi was infatuated with the advertising manager of the *Hutchinson News*, Harry C. Williams. The story that she never confirmed or denied was that a coin was tossed to determine who she would wed. The coin favored Williams, and he led her to the altar.

This marriage was not to be long-lived, however. After a few weeks, she informed Harry that he was not keeping her in the lifestyle that she was used to nor expected. After a few weeks, Sidi headed to Los Angeles and was performing in a night club when she met sugar multimillionaire John D. Spreckles II. John had seen her singing and dancing in the club and was immediately infatuated with her. He was married and had to wait for his divorce to become final before he wed Sidi.

Together, John and Sidi had one daughter, Geraldine. Before Geraldine was very old, John wrecked his automobile and was killed. There was a battle over the estate, of which his father, John Spreckles Sr., became administrator. The estate awarded Sidi $24,000 since the child of John Jr. was a minor.

Sidi was involved in the Hollywood scene and befriended a young actress named Miss Virginia Rapp. Rapp had been at a party in Rosco "Fatty" Arbuckle's rooms at the St. Francis Hotel in San Francisco. Fatty Arbuckle was one of the silent screen's largest stars, literally and professionally. Fatty carried the nearly unconscious actress to another room and laid her on the bed. A doctor was summoned, as was the hotel manager. The semiconscious woman was taken to a hospital, where she lived for three days before dying.

A physician pronounced her as having had "too much liquor." There were no visible signs of trauma, although the autopsy showed massive internal injuries. Sidi was called to testify at the series of trials. Sidi had a few words with Rapp before she died. A series of accusations from a known woman who had a history of blackmail and an overambitious district attorney put the famous actor through three trials before a not guilty verdict was produced. Details of the party have been debated, but it was enough to create a firestorm of emotions about the Hollywood culture and gave rise to the Hollywood Censorship Board. It also ruined Fatty's career.

Sidi next made headlines by marrying Prince Suad Bey Chakir of Turkey. The headlines all over the nation announced how a rancher's daughter from Garden City had now become a Turkish princess. The prince lived in the finest house in Turkey, and Sidi fell into a life of wealth and influence that she had not had before. She was in France when another Turkish prince was shot by his wife. Prince Chakir was a member of a progressive group, and women were finding new freedoms under the influence of the prince and many contemporaries. The family was an old and ancient line. It was said that Sidi was the mistress of riches, chatelaine of one of the most luxurious homes in Constantinople, as well as a summer home on an island off the coast of Turkey. A statement by the *San Francisco Chronicle* noted that "this is the standing today of the beautiful and strangely magnetic woman whose life has been replete with romance and adventure."

Life as a princess was not what it appeared to be, and soon Sidi was back in the United States and living at a ranch near Reno, Nevada, in order to qualify as a resident for at least thirty days for a quick divorce. In order to get her citizenship back, she had to go before a federal judge, who asked her if she was prepared to renounce her Turkish citizenship, to which she replied, "I have already done that." When asked if she would renounce her title as a princess, she smiled and said yes.

During her time at the ranch in Reno, there were U.S. Army aviators who flew over quite often; the women living there would wave at the flyers, and the flyers would wave back. One of these aviators was Lieutenant Roger Gardner, the son of the Gardner family of San Francisco. A romance developed, much to the chagrin of the Gardner family.

An order for Gardner's transfer to Langley Field in Virginia led the Gardner family to believe this would put an end to the romance. However, Sidi took her daughter and headed for Fairfax, Virginia, and she and Roger

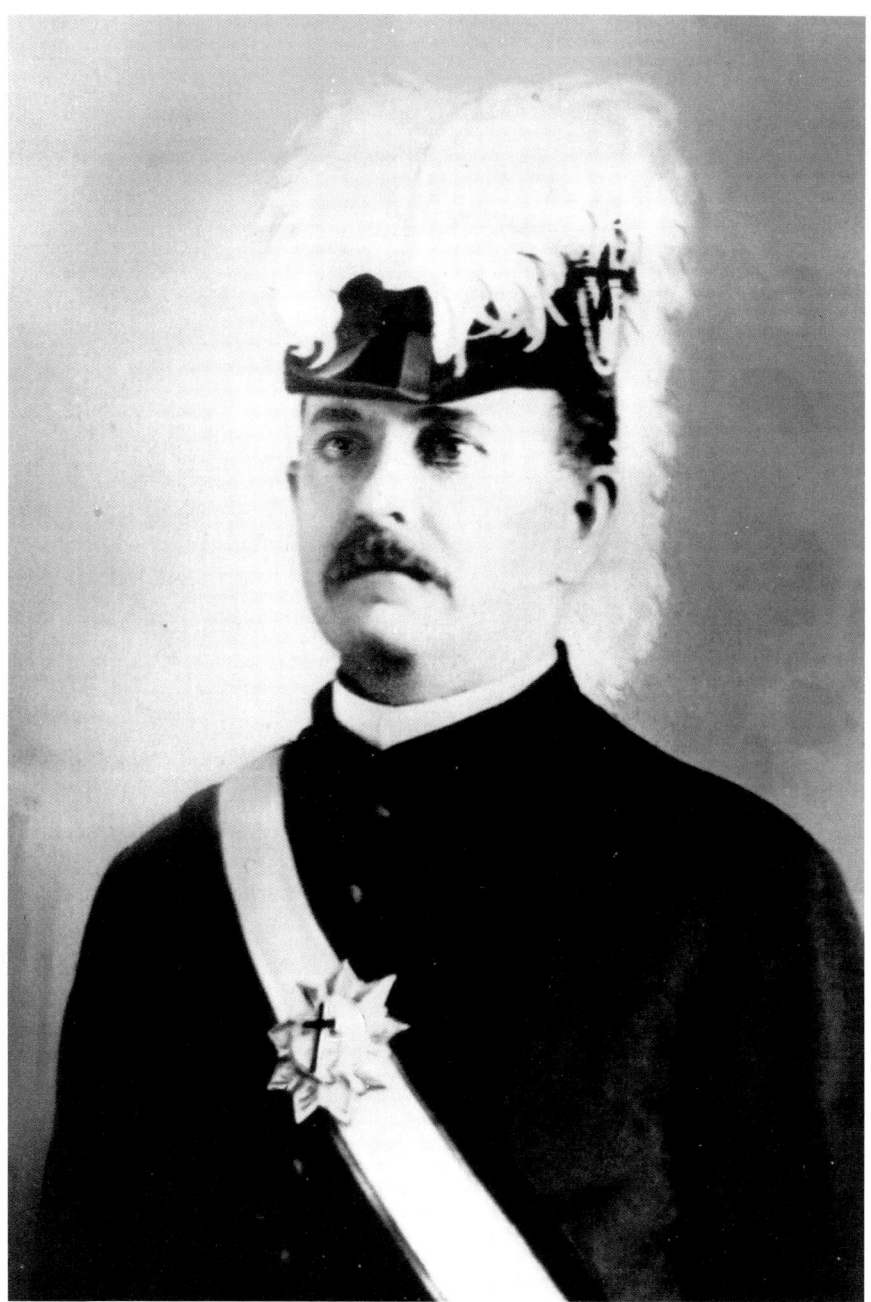

E.L. (Edward) Wirt. *Courtesy of Finney County Historical Museum.*

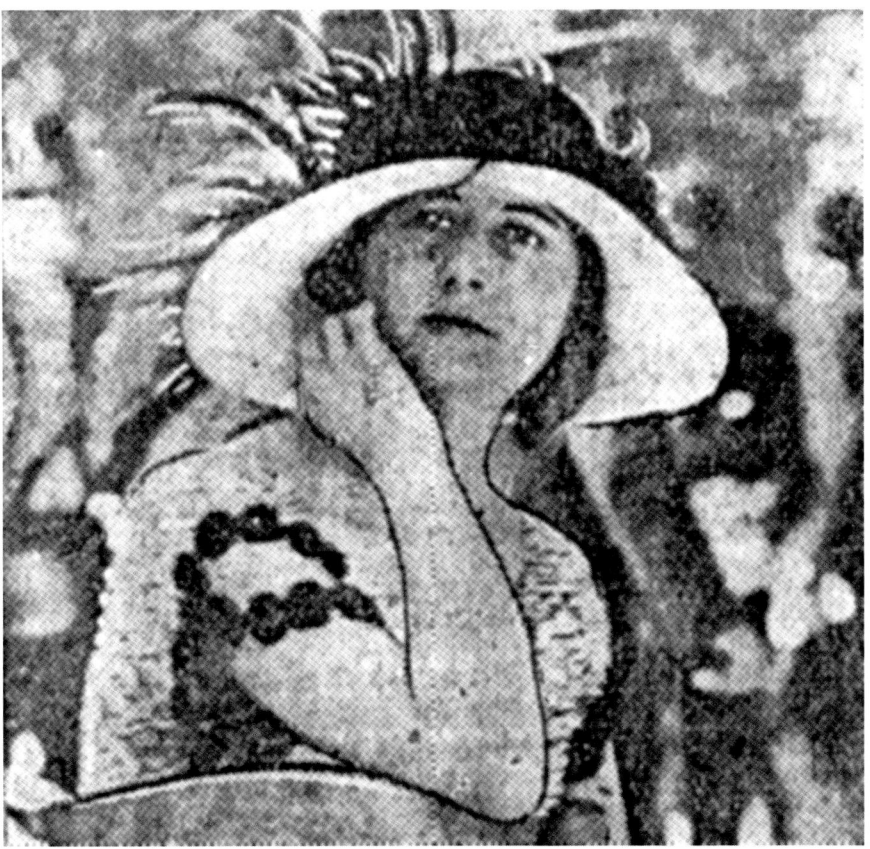

Sydia Wirt Spreckles, circa 1920s. *Courtesy of Finney County Historical Museum.*

were married before a judge. The newspapers thought that the marriage would not have any chance. The couple wed in 1929, and with the exception of an accident that her daughter had when she was severely burned, there is no record on how the couple spent their life.

The last place that newspapers placed Sidi as living was in El Paso, Texas. There is a gap from the early 1930s onward until a death certificate was found for Sydia Wirt Spreckles. She is listed as a housewife but had spent several years in a hospital and died of cerebral arteriosclerosis on June 1, 1970, in Dallas, Texas. She was listed as widowed. As for the grave in which she is supposed to be buried, the State of Texas has no record of her being there.

UTOPIA COLLEGE

Utopia, Kansas, has very little to set it apart besides being listed as a ghost town. The small town near Eureka in Greenwood County never had a large influx of settlers. Its post office was started in 1880 and lasted until 1935. It never was a big town. There was one thing, however, that distinguished the town: it lent its name to Reverend Roger Babson as the name for the college he opened in Eureka.

Babson believed that the threat of atomic warfare was so great that the most likely place to survive a nuclear war was centered on Eureka, Kansas, so he built his third institution there in 1946 and later took the name of Utopia for the college. Babson was an economist and philanthropist, and his economic theory led him to place Eureka in the center of what is called "Babson's Magic Circle." It was composed of what he called the "most underpopulated breadbasket of the earth," which includes parts of Iowa, Missouri, Arkansas, Oklahoma and Kansas. He theorized that the resources of the area could easily support 60 million people in luxury and 150 million people in an emergency.

His concern was that the twelve largest cities in the United States would be the targets for nuclear bombs and that, at that time, 20 percent of the population of the country lived in those places. He recognized that people would have to be fed, fueled and reorganized by the people living in the central part of the nation.

The Utopia College offered students a certificate program but not a diploma for a two-year session. Graduates were recommended to complete undergraduate work at the two Babson colleges located elsewhere in the country. Babson College later changed its name to the Midwest Institute of Business Administration. After declining enrollment, the colleges closed permanently in 1970.

Utopia College in Eureka was originally intended to be built underground, although this never happened. Babson purchased an entire block in Eureka, which consisted of about three acres. Existing homes were converted into the college's headquarters, and area homes were purchased to house students.

Walter A. Bowers, a business instructor at the University of Kansas, was hired to head the college. The school opened in 1947. Babson and Bowers spoke to area groups, promoting the school and expanding on their doomsday scenario. Even with his belief in the scenario, Babson never relocated to Eureka to live. Babson stayed at his home in New Boston, New Hampshire (presently named Manchester).

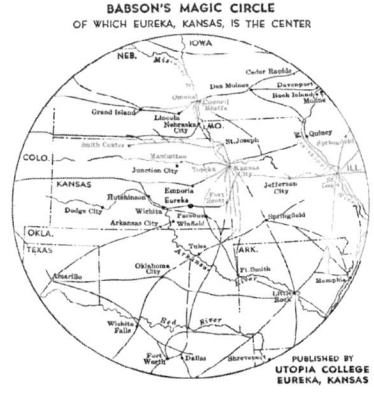
Utopia College, Babson's Magic Circle.
Courtesy of Babson College.

The school never grew to what Babson envisioned, and he died in 1967. The board of directors closed down the Midwest Institute (all three locations) in 1970. The other two campuses were located in Massachusetts and Florida. The original building still stands in Eureka and is now privately owned. An exhibit can be seen telling the story of Utopia College in the Greenwood County Historical Museum in Eureka.

As a side note, if you put the name of Roger Babson in a search engine, you will find a lot of information on the relative Roger W. Babson, for whom he was named. A historical sign in Eureka tells the story of Roger Babson, who was burned at the stake in 1555 in England for translating the Bible into English.

INDIAN CHARLEY

In his youth, Charles Curtis was called "Indian Charley," born near Topeka on January 25, 1860, while Kansas was still a territory. His mother, Ellen Papin, was one-fourth Kaw, one-fourth Osage, one-fourth Potawatomi and one-fourth French. His father, Owen Curtis, was English, Scottish and Welsh. On his mother's side, Charley was descended from Chief White Plume (Kaw) and Pawhuska (Osage). His first languages were Kansa and French, which he learned from his mother. His mother died when he was three, so he lived on the Kaw Reservation and returned to them in later years.

Charley had a passion for racing horses and was a successful jockey running prairie races. When he was eight years old, on June 1, 1868, the

Cheyennes invaded the Kaw Reservation, causing the white settlers in the area to flee to Council Grove for protection. The Kaw warriors painted their faces, donned their regalia and rode out to confront the Cheyennes. The rivals put on a superb display of horsemanship, with war cries and volleys of arrows and bullets. During the battle, a mixed-blood scout named Joe Jim rode to Topeka for assistance from the governor, and by his side rode Indian Charley. However, after four hours on the battlefield, there were no casualties, and with a few stolen horses and offerings of coffee and sugar from Council Grove merchants, the Cheyennes withdrew.

Charley's father fought in the Civil War and was taken captive. During this time, Charley's maternal grandparents helped him gain possession of his mother's property in North Topeka. The Kaw society was matriarchal, and inheritance flowed through the mother to the son. His father tried unsuccessfully to gain the property.

Both sets of grandparents were very supportive about education. After living on the reservation, Charley returned to Topeka and went to Topeka High School. Upon graduation, he worked for an established law firm and read for the law. He was admitted to the bar, practiced law in Topeka and served as a prosecuting attorney from 1885 to 1889.

Applying the same enthusiasm for horses and racing to politics, Charles was elected to the First District seat in the House of Representatives as a Republican. One of the bills he sponsored and helped pass was the Curtis Act of 1898, which extended the Davis Act to the five civilized tribes of the Oklahoma Territory. Based on personal experience, he believed that the tribes would benefit by education, assimilation and joining mainstream society. Implementation of the act extinguished tribal land titles in Indian Territory, preparing it for statehood, which happened in 1907. The government tried to get Indians to accept individual citizenship and land. The government had set up boarding schools by the end of the nineteenth century. The Kaw tribe had been moved to Indian Territory via the 1902 Kaw Allotment Act, and the nation was disbanded as a legal entity. Curtis was an enrolled member and received 1.625 acres for himself and his three children.

Charles and House member Daniel Read Anthony (First District representative for Kansas and Charles's successor, as he had been appointed to the Senate) sponsored the first Equal Rights Amendment. Charles was elected Republican Senate whip and majority leader from 1925 to 1929. He was considered to be one of the best political poker players and a great reconciler. Of course, you should recognize by now that Indian Charley

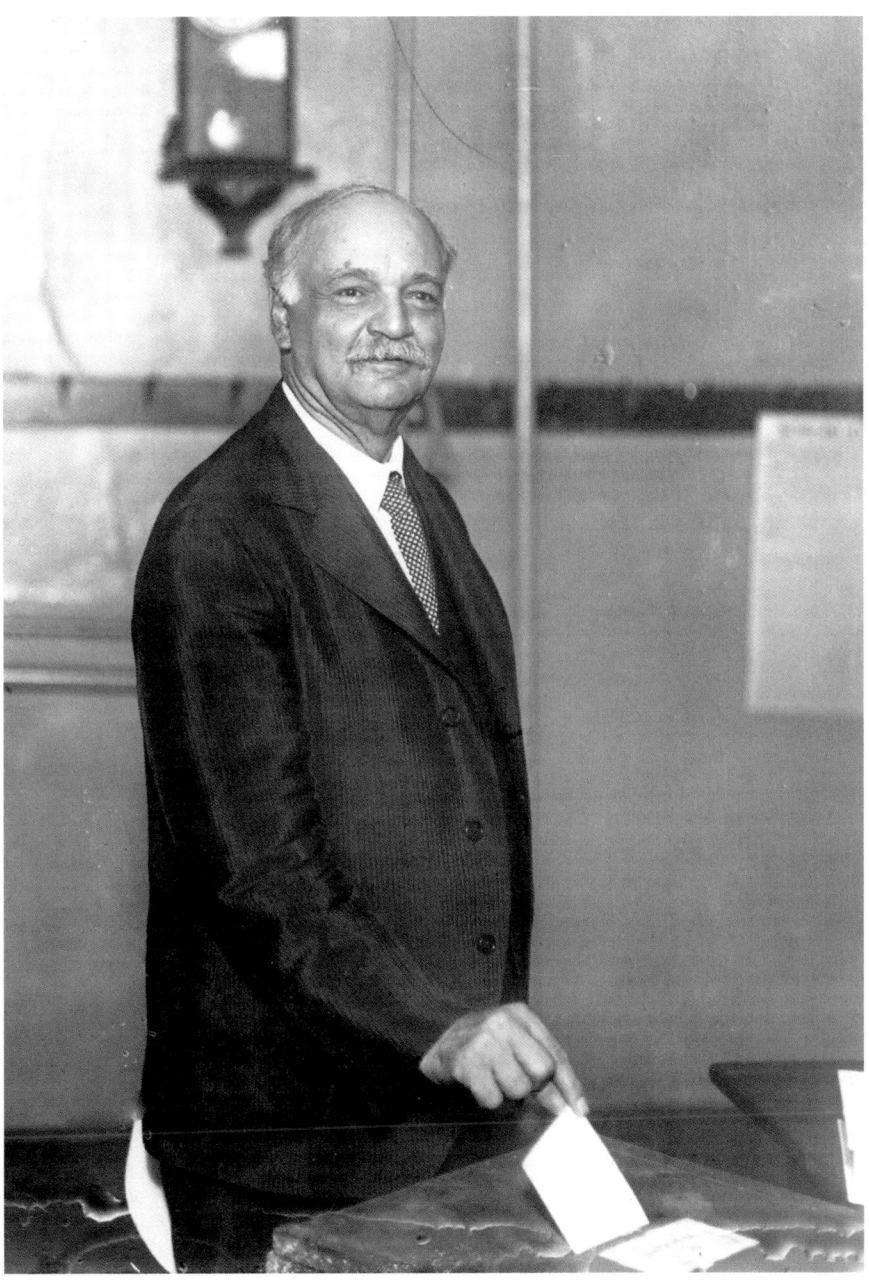

Charles Curtis, first Native American vice-president of the United States. *Courtesy of Kansas State Historical Society.*

is Charles Curtis. Charles went on to win a landslide victory with Herbert Hoover as vice-president of the United States. The win was 58 percent to 41 percent. At his inauguration, Charles arranged for a Native American jazz band to play. He was the first vice-president to be sworn into office on a bible as the president is. After the Depression began, he supported the five-day workweek with no reduction of wages as a solution for unemployment. He was sixty-nine when elected to the vice-presidency. Curtis was not a great orator or speech maker but was known for his meticulous set of index cards. He wrote down every person's name he met and had a remarkable memory. Every letter he received was promptly answered.

Curtis was the first to employ a female secretary. Mrs. Lola Williams of Columbus had worked for Curtis for some time and was one of the first women to enter the floor of the Senate. The voters, however, decided that the Hoover administration had not done enough to solve the Depression, and Hoover lost the bid for a second term. Curtis had married and had three children (his wife was deceased). A half-sister had come to live with the family—Theresa Permillia "Dolly" Curtis served as his hostess for social events. Curtis was the last vice-president who remained unmarried throughout his term of office. He stayed in Washington practicing law and died there on February 8, 1936. He is buried beside his wife in Topeka.

AMERICA'S FIRST PATENTED HELICOPTER

Traveling down I-70, it would be a good idea to stop at the High Plains Museum in Goodland. The museum commissioned Harold Newton, a Brewster pilot and mechanic, to build a working replica of the first patented helicopter in America. Some may stop here and suggest that the first patent was from Sikorsky, but this would be an incorrect statement. Igor Sikorsky was responsible for building the VS-300 helicopter on September 14, 1939 (its first tethered test) and carries the recognition for the "first practical helicopter." To label it the first *patented* would not be correct. In the 1930s, there was another helicopter patented by Marriage, originally from Mullinville.

The honor of the first patent for a helicopter goes to William J. Purvis. In 1909, Purvis saw a child playing with a whirligig in a candy store. The railroad mechanic saw the idea for a flying machine. He gave the child a penny and left with the toy. This is a theme that plays itself out time

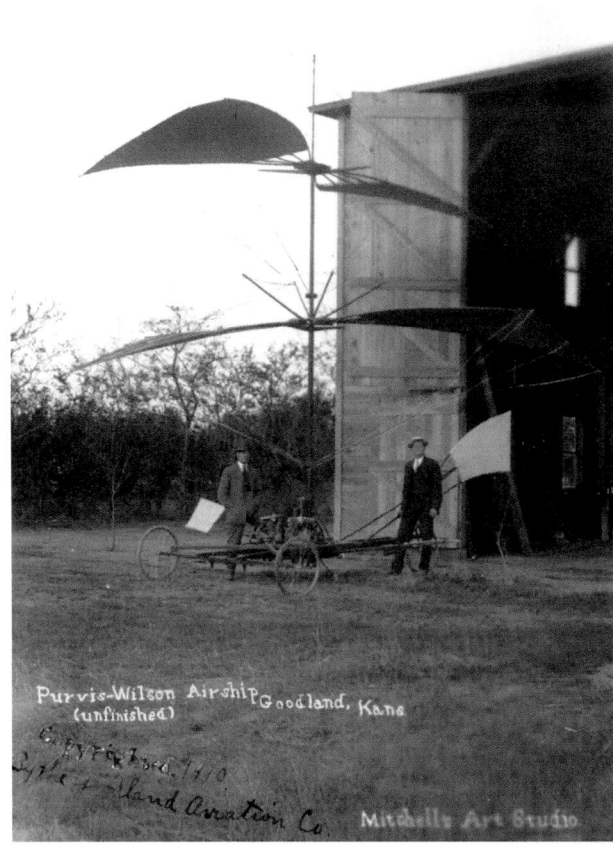

First helicopter patented. *Courtesy of High Plains Museum, Goodland, Kansas.*

and again in Kansas history: seemingly ordinary things seem to catch the attention of an active mind with an imagination and an invention or improvement takes hold.

On Thanksgiving Day 1909, a crowd gathered to watch a demonstration of Purvis and his partner Charles A. Wilson's gyrocopter. Although weighed down with rocks to prevent flight, the machine lifted off the ground before settling back down. The demonstrator had been powered with a six-horsepower gas engine.

Purvis announced that $10 shares would be sold in the new Goodland Aviation Company. Shares were sold at a local lawyer's office. Investors paid $30,000 for stock in the company. This is quite a feat considering that the average yearly wage was from $200 to $400.

A workshop and hangar was built at what is now the intersection of Highway 24 and Cattletrail Road in Goodland. The gyrocopter was terribly underpowered, so Purvis traveled to St. Louis to buy a larger model, but he did not have enough funds to buy it. By this time, investors were growing skeptical and refused to infuse more money into the operation. Had the new motor been obtained, there were still problems of providing enough lift and controlling torque.

The pair did make progress that would eventually lead to practical helicopters. The model had a counter rotator, which was an early breakthrough in practical helicopter design. In March 1911, however, Goodland Aviation disbanded and sold its assets. Both men left Goodland, never to meet again. In 1912, the U.S. Patent Office granted patent no. 1,028,781, but by this time it was too late for the gyrocopter to have a chance to fly.

At the High Plains Museum, the replica built by Harold Norton is mounted on a pedestal. By pushing a button on a counter, the motor will start and the rotors turn. The public cannot get into the well with the model without special permission. A visit by a great-nephew of Purvis allowed the relative to get down and examine the machine his predecessor designed. The family has many of the original pictures of the gyrocopter. Had time and funds not been limited, the history of flight may have taken a somewhat different path at an earlier time.

MAYRATH

Mayrath is a familiar name in agriculture, specifically the grain auger business. The Mayraths were very early settlers in Ford County, Kansas. The family was the first to stake a claim in Fairview Township, which was about seven miles southwest of Dodge City. Nicholas Mayrath was a farmer and gardener from Illinois and made a success of his farm. Willing to do more work than many neighbors would do, he started selling produce and farm products in Dodge City. Weathering the droughty conditions and other conditions of western Kansas, he managed to accumulate ten quarters of ground.

His son, Martin, continued his work, and he had a son also named Martin. Handling grain was a hard manual process using scoop shovels. In 1943, Martin Jr. invented a grain auger. He received a patent on it in 1945. Soldiers returning home from World War II were quick to recognize that

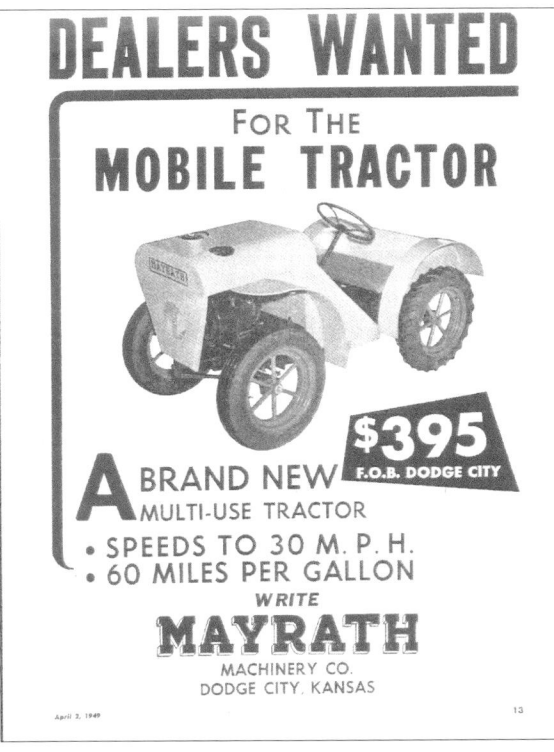

Left: "Dealers Wanted" advertisement for Mayrath Tractors. *Courtesy of Harvey Fox.*

Below: Deluxe Model, Mayrath tractor. *Courtesy of Harvey Fox.*

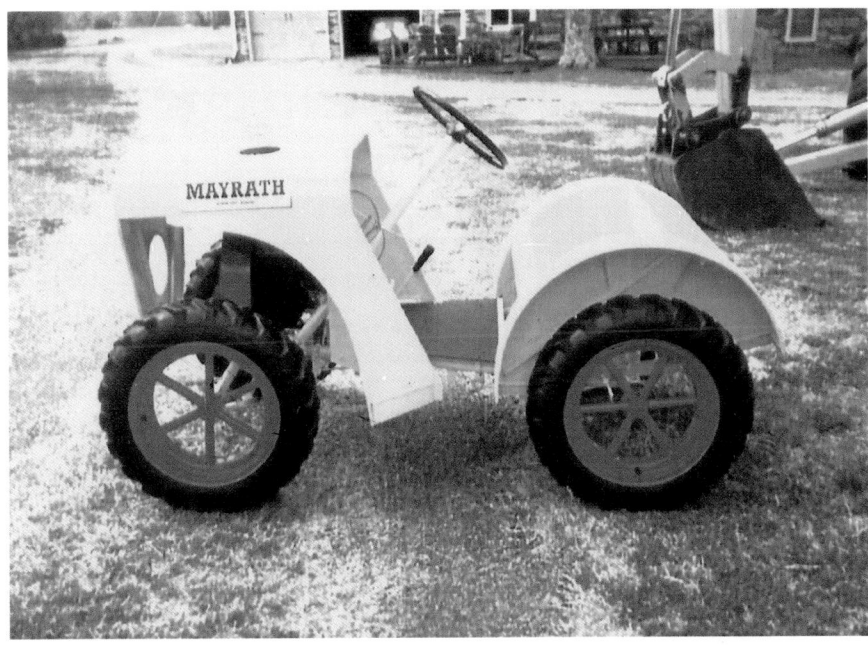

the improvement of farming technology increases the volume of grain that needs to be handled.

Mayrath found a demand for his product and built a manufacturing facility in Dodge City. The company rapidly grew, and with that growth came ideas for other products. From 1949 until 1952, the company built a small tractor. Considered a garden tractor by today's standards, two models were built: the Standard, which featured no sheet metal, and the Deluxe, which had a hood and fenders.

The tractors were powered by a Briggs & Stratton 8.25-horsepower engine. Two selling points were a top speed of thirty miles per hour and a range of sixty miles on one gallon of gas. The tractors are very desirable for collectors today, listed in tractor books as a defunct product (this did not deter the success of the company).

The company went on to build a facility in Illinois and was eventually bought out by Hutchinson Manufacturing. Headquarters for the company became Clay Center, Kansas. Through later acquisitions, the Hutchinson/Mayrath Company is part of Global Industries, headquartered in Grand Island, Nebraska.

In 1998, the Hutchinson/Mayrath Company expanded the Clay Center facility, and today about four hundred are employed by the company.

DUANE NELSON: COWBOY

A mainstay at Old Cowtown Museum for many years could be seen walking the streets, rope in hand, educating and entertaining the visitors—especially the kids—about what he called the "Cowboys of Color." Duane called himself a black cowboy, but others would call him African American. The author knew him as a dedicated educator who had come up through life with many of the same difficulties faced by others.

Born in Oklahoma on June 21, 1941, he grew up in the area east of Oklahoma City and worked as a cowboy on small outfits around the region. Duane completed work at the Oklahoma Farriers College, the first black man to do so. This was at a time when it was determined that he would not get through it. After completion, he was offered a position as an instructor at the school. He worked as a farrier for about four years.

Coming to Wichita, he participated in the early civil rights sit-in protests at Dockums Drug Store lunch counter. He came to Old Wichita Cowtown

Museum after retiring from Derby Refining Company. He came to Old Cowtown as a lead interpreter and security. Living on the property, he immersed himself in the life of the original replica of Wichita that depicted the time from 1865 to 1880.

In a story published in *American Cowboy Magazine* by this author in 1998, Duane maintained that he felt an obligation to tell the truth about the past. His story, the story of the black cowboy, was a major part of the estimated thirty-five thousand drovers who moved the cattle up the trails from Texas to markets in the North. He not only told the stories, but he was also an avid researcher and built a reference library on the individuals who, for the most part, are lost to standard western history.

The setting at Old Cowtown was a perfect vehicle for Duane to share the stories. A fellow worker, Dave "Prairie Dog" Lafferty, commented on Duane's easygoing nature that could hold the attention of the most distracted visitor. Duane delighted in taking the "Cowboy Program" to Wichita and area schools. His friendly nature always enchanted the weekly visitors from a tour bus company out of New York that was at the museum every Friday with foreign and East Coast visitors.

Duane's friend Ernie Fullerton, a horse trainer and trader, said that "Duane is one of the finest people I've ever known." He went on to say that

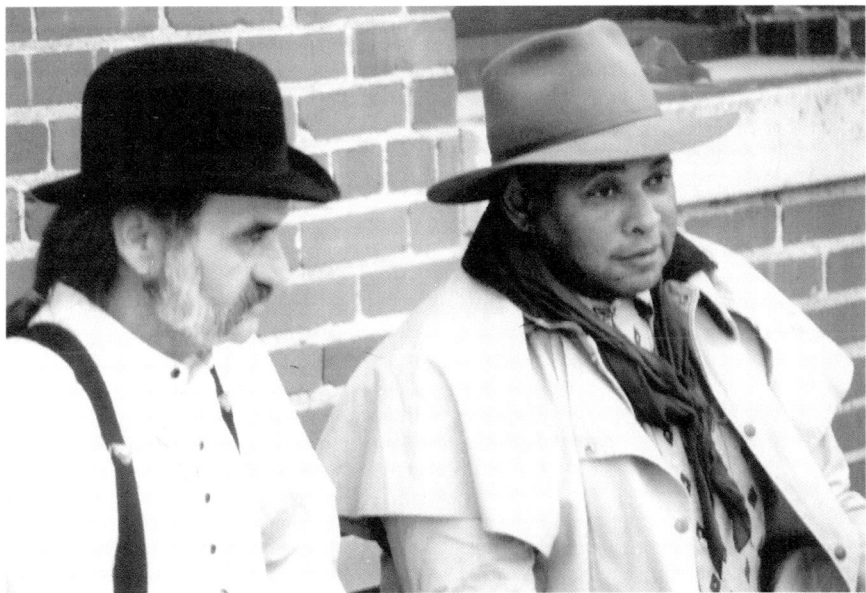

Duane Nelson with Dave Lafferty. *Photo by Roger Ringer.*

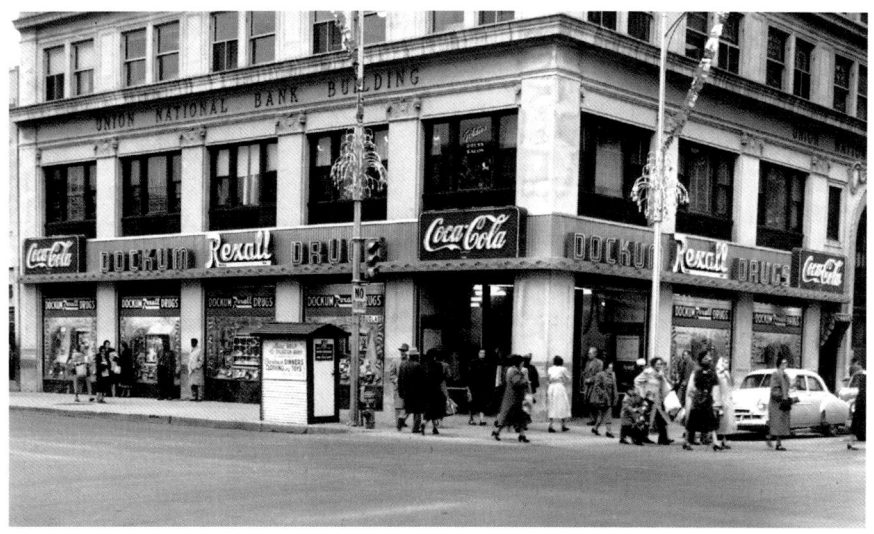

Dockums Drug Store, scene of civil rights sit-in. *Courtesy of Wichita-Sedgwick County Historical Museum.*

he enjoyed everything that he has read of Duane's poetry, "and he can throw a loop better than anyone I have ever seen."

Duane was encouraged with his cowboy poetry writing by folklorist and Kansas cowboy Dr. Jim Hoy. Hoy included a few of Duane's poems in his anthology "Prairie Poetry: Cowboy Verse of Kansas" (*Wichita Eagle*, 1995). Duane participated in the Cowboy Heritage Festival in Dodge City and the National Cowboy Symposium in Lubbock, Texas.

Duane worked with the author and Dave Lafferty on a television production concept for public broadcasting called *Cowboys, Plowboys, and Country Folk*. The project was considered to be one of the best proposals for new programming at the local affiliate, but lack of funding prevented the show from going into production.

After retiring from Old Cowtown, Duane returned quite often as a volunteer. He also worked for several years for the African American Museum in Wichita. His delight was always working with kids, especially African American, as he can show them their western heritage.

Duane was a regular in productions that used the authentic setting of Cowtown for everything from movies to commercials. He was an extra in the movie *Stolen Women*, starring Janine Turner.

Duane commented on his ability to educate kids, saying "they are interested and it was fun." Duane died on January 21, 2015.

TERESA CUEVAS: MARIACHI ESTRELLA DE TOPEKA

Teresa Cuevas was born in Topeka in 1920. Her parents had fled to Kansas during the Mexican Revolution. As a child, she studied the violin. Being married and divorced in a male-dominated culture, Teresa was a vigorous person and raised four sons and a daughter. She always stressed "that her ideals being challenged made her do what she thought she was capable of." Little did she know what her drive and talent would push her to become.

This Our Lady of Guadalupe church member became a fixture in the mariachi world when Teresa founded an all-female mariachi band. Mariachi Estrella de Topeka was the first such mariachi band in the United States. The group soon became a regional favorite. Its members were Connie "Chae" Alcala, Dolores "Lola" Carmona, Delores "Lola Galvin" Sangalang, Isabel "Bole" Gonzales, Linda Scurlock and Teresa Cuevas.

The group was at the height of its popularity in 1980 and 1981. Then tragedy struck. On July 17, 1981, the group was to play for a corporate gathering and was on the skywalks at the Hyatt Regency Center when the walks collapsed; 114 people were killed in the collapse and 200 were injured. Teresa was among the injured and was trapped under rubble for hours. She recalled a man near her asking what happened, and eventually his voice faded away and he died.

Four members of the group died that day: Delores Galvin, Connie Alcala, Dolores Carmona and Linda Rokey Scurlock. These members are memorialized on a historical marker located in Topeka. The marker is on Southeast Quincy Street near Eighth Avenue. The memorial is on the west grounds of the Topeka Performing Arts Center. The music lived on through the members left behind.

On January 5, 2009, a press release from the Kansas Humanities Council awarded a grant to Justia Inc. Topeka for the creation of a documentary featuring the story of Mariachi Estrella de Topeka. Marlo Angell was the project director. The documentary was shown on television stations throughout the region and is a tribute to a great group that serves as inspiration to many people today.

Teresa would have another major heartbreak in her life when on May 11, 1996, her granddaughter Marlo Cuevas-Balandran was killed aboard ValuJet Flight 592 when it crashed into the Florida Everglades. When she died, Marlo was pursuing a career in Mexican music.

Teresa played her violin well into her eighties and was an inspiration for everyone in the area. She motivated countless women and men through her violin playing and her performances. She played as long as she could at the annual Mexican Fiesta at Our Lady of Guadalupe Church in Topeka. It was one of her favorite times of the year. She always played for family gatherings and had her grandchildren accompany her.

Teresa died on December 12, 2013, at the age of ninety-three. She will always be considered an extraordinary person and a proud resident of this state.

LAWRIN: KENTUCKY DERBY WINNER

It is as improbable as any story in horse racing. Kansas is not thought of as a contributor to the top Thoroughbred racing horses in the world. There have been many quarter horses and Appaloosa racing champions bred and raised in this state, but a Kentucky Derby champion is not what anyone would think of when you mention Kansas horse racing. But there was one.

A Kansas City merchant with a love of horse racing purchased a horse named Insco in 1933 for $500. Insco was the son of a great sire by the name of Sir Gallahad III. Insco would sire a number of successful stakes winners, including Lawrin, and herein lies the story. Lawrin was the least likely winner of a major race, according to the experts of the time. It was a special set of circumstances and special people coming together that made history in 1938 at the sixty-fourth running of the Kentucky Derby.

The owner was Kansas City businessman Herbert M. Woolf. Mr. Woolf owned the Woolf Brothers Clothing stores, which his father and uncle had started in Lawrence, Kansas. The business was moved to Kansas City and then, under the guidance of Herbert, expanded to multiple locations, including Wichita. Herbert owned Woolford Farm, which has now been grown over by the city of Prairie Village.

Woolford Farm was the retreat for Herbert, where he would entertain guests such as Teddy Roosevelt and Tom Pendergast. It was also where he indulged in his passion and love of racing horses. He also had a registered herd of Hereford cattle. Paying $500 for Insco soon would pay off in a big way when Lawrin was born. Woolf engaged the services of hall of fame horse trainer Ben A. Jones.

Jones had Lawrin in Florida but brought the horse to Kentucky to take a shot at the Derby. Jones was trying to get jockey Wayne Wright to ride the colt, but he had a prior commitment to ride Caballero in the Excelsior Handicap in New York on the same day as the Derby, a race he did win. Jones contacted an up-and-coming jockey and offered the ride to him, even though he had never been on the horse before. That jockey was hall of famer Eddie Arcaro. Arcaro had been riding for Green Tree, and he was sure he could get permission to ride but had his own misgivings, hearing whispers from Florida that Lawrin might not be sound.

Jones was persistent, and Arcaro was engaged to ride the race. Jones said to Arcaro several times that "he'll give you an eighth in eleven seconds any time you make a move with him." Keeping this in mind, and conscious of the position on the rail that could become a trap, Arcaro held position back. Not knowing how much horse he had under him, he made the move, roared to the front and won the race.

Today, the graves and monuments of Insco and Lawrin are at the site of the old Woolford Farm in a housing addition in Prairie Village. This seems a fitting monument to the great Kansas horses responsible for "bringing home the roses" to Kansas.

HAP PEEBLES: ENTERTAINMENT ICON

Hap Peebles was a youth in Anthony when he started learning to work hard and develop a drive to succeed. Born in 1913 in Anthony, his father was a clerk and mechanic at the local hardware store. Hap worked summers for area farmers and became a delivery boy for the *Anthony Republican* newspaper. He later became a reporter for the *Anthony Republican*.

Hap played basketball in Anthony and attended Anthony Christian Church. Getting an early start in entertainment, he worked for O.F. Fletcher, who was secretary of the Anthony Fair and Race Association and the Kansas-Oklahoma-Missouri Trotting Horse Association. Hap served as publicity director for both organizations in the 1920s. Graduating in 1931 from Anthony High School, he became a sports reporter for the *Anthony Republican* and started to organize concerts for Anthony and surrounding towns. The first act he worked with was Bob Wills, legendary Texas bandleader.

Moving to Wichita, he worked as a sports reporter for the *Wichita Eagle* and continued to promote concerts. He also promoted sporting events. He would promote country and western shows, rodeos, circuses and theater.

Hap helped Ray Dumont elevate the semiprofessional National Baseball Congress, founded in 1934. Hap was commissioner for many of the districts and advanced tournaments. He joined the congress staff in 1945, serving as editor and public relations officer. He started a full-time public relations agency in 1948. In 1962, Hap handled the touring schedule for the Negro American League Kansas City Monarchs. At this same time, while working with the baseball congress, promoting events and concerts, he was officiating basketball and football games. The basketball teams were from the amateur independent leagues, which were sponsored by area businesses. He was involved with the Southern Kansas Independent Basketball Association and with the Missouri Valley AAU Committee as tournament director. He also was an umpire.

Hap had a gentle demeanor and a quiet voice and put others' needs before his own. His signature was a big white cowboy hat, and he stood behind the curtain for many acts, from Bob Wills and the Texas Playboys to Eddie Arnold, Barbara Mandrel and Alabama. With an early partner, Ben Truex, Hap pioneered the concept of bringing the Grand Ole Opry tours and many other acts to Wichita and the region. With Kansas long considered "fly-over country," Hap made it a destination. Acts would tour county fairs, the state fair, festivals and many other venues.

Loving the industry and wanting it to flourish, Hap always put the interests of the attendees first and the artists second. He never let an act go without pay even when he did not make a dime. He wanted the experience for both fans and artists to be top priority. He had revolutionary ideas and did things like book country acts with rock-and-roll acts in the same shows.

It was not unusual for artists to get stiffed by promoters if things did not go right, and this was something that Hap fought against. He always thought that there should be stability in the industry and that honesty was a casualty sometimes—he was against that. He was at the foundation meeting of the Country Music Association with Hubert Long in 1958. In 1970, he was founder of the International Country Buyers Association with fellow promoter Don Romero. Hap sat at the head of the table for the ICBA for twenty-three years as president, executive director and chairman of the board for life, until his death in 1993. He was also serving on the CMA Board of Directors for fifteen years, was awarded the CMA's first SRO Award in 1985 and was considered for its hall of fame. The ICBA honored his contributions in 2011, awarding him the Robert E. Mallory Award of Excellence and inducting him into its hall of fame in 2010. He received the

1997 Hap Peebles Award, and in 1991, a scholarship at Belmont University was endowed in his name.

Hap booked most of his shows within hours of his Wichita and Kansas City offices. As a trailblazer, he connected artists with fairs across the Midwest and was named South Dakota Fair Man of the Year in 1976, Iowa Fair Man in 1977, Event Person of the Year by the North Dakota Association of Fairs in 1979, Associate of the Year by Nebraska Fair Association in 1979, Service Member of the Year by the Rocky Mountain Association of Fairs in 1981, Hall of Fame North Dakota Association of Fairs in 1984, Colorado Outstanding Associate Member in 1986, Louisiana Association of Fairs and Festival Hall of Fame in 1991 and Hall of Fame member of the Iowa Fairs in 1992. He was also inducted into the halls of fame for Arkansas, Wyoming, Montana, Kansas and Oklahoma.

Hap was the first to arrange shows in prisons, and the acts were all volunteers. He started in the Nebraska Penitentiary in 1962 with Roy Acuff and George Morgan and then went to the Kansas State Penitentiary and the U.S. Federal Penitentiary in Leavenworth. After the Topeka tornado in 1966, he organized an eleven-hour marathon. Hap lost tens of thousands of dollars when the roof was torn off a venue in Topeka where he had a show lined up, and he also lost his Topeka office during the tornado.

As part of the work of promoting shows, the radio stations were very important. Hap had great working relationships and personal friendships with radio station owners, DJs and station employees. Always original, the Grand Ole Opry Show at the Forum in Wichita was the scene for one of his most unusual events in 1952. The show consisted of Tex Ritter, Hank Morgan, Carl Perkins, the Plainsmen Quartet, the LeGarde twins (from Australia), Moon Mullican, Gary Van and His Western Starlighters, Hawkshaw Hawkins and Miss Jean Sheppard. Hawkshaw Hawkins and Jean Sheppard were the center of attention. After the show, Hap promoted the largest hillbilly wedding since Hank Williams was married on stage in Shreveport, Louisiana, seven years before. Congratulations for Hawkins and Sheppard came in from Governor Jimmie Davis, Chet Atkins and Opry members.

Miss Sheppard wore a wedding gown and was escorted through the audience by Mack Sanders (local owner of KSIR radio), who emceed the wedding. Hap gave Jean away. The wedding was broadcast on radio up to the exchanging of vows. The audience was invited to stay and partake in wedding cake and a souvenir off the arbor. The cake lasted for one thousand people. It was another stroke of genius for Hap and his love of providing a great experience for the fans and artists.

The Hap Peebles Agency office in Wichita was located north of Kellogg on Seneca Street on the east side. This would be just south of Maple. Hap went out on his own after the death of partner William Floto in 1948, who was a businessman and theatrical agent in Wichita. Hap was friends with virtually every name in the music business. Hap died in Kansas City on January 8, 1993. He is buried at White Chapel Memorial Gardens in Wichita.

SEXY REXY: REX ALLEN PYEATT

For many years if you went to a rodeo in south-central Kansas, the clown who would be working the crowd and protecting the cowboys was very likely Sexy Rexy. Working for many years for the Carpenter Rodeo Company, he would keep things light and people laughing throughout the performances with his antics. There is always a story behind the greasepaint and funny clothes, and Sexy Rexy in real life was Rex Allen Pyeatt.

Rex was named after the cowboy star and singer Rex Allen, and he grew up in the Mulvane area in the 1950s. The family moved to town, but the farm was kept and even added to. When Rex was eight years old, he was with his father planting wheat. Everything was going fine until he reached his gloved hand down to check the wheat coming out of the drill. His gloved hand got caught and was pulled into the gears. His father managed to get the hand out. He wrapped the mangled hand in rags that were in the truck and drove to the hospital, where they put a metal rod in his thumb. He ended up with usage of only 80 percent of the hand.

Therapy in those days consisted of a bucket filled with rocks that Rex would lift in order to get his hand working again and strengthen it. The accident caused him to miss half of his third grade year, so he had to repeat the year of schooling. He learned to live with the disability, and chores were still a part of his life afterward.

In Rex's high school years, he became interested in rodeo. He became a member of the FFA and was very active in the organization. He tried riding broncs and bulls, but his hand made things too difficult to go ahead with this in high school. After graduation, he went to Cheyenne Wyoming Frontier Days Rodeo, which had been a dream of his all his life. It was there that Rex had the idea of becoming a rodeo clown. Coming back home, he contacted

Norman Carpenter of Carpenter Rodeo Company. Norman agreed to take him on, and his rodeo clown career began. Rex was famous for the modified car named Bullford that was used in his shows.

The Carpenter Rodeo Company did shows all over the central Kansas and Oklahoma areas. Many people watched the antics of Sexy Rexy over the years. During this time, he met a barrel racer named Janet Purdy, and she became the love of his life. They started a family—Talon, Ty and Nikki. They watched Rex perform for many years. Age finally gave him the hint that it was time to give up entertaining and protecting cowboys in the rodeo.

There is a railroad crossing near Rex's farm close to Mulvane. At a certain angle at the wrong time in the morning, the sun blinded Rex to an oncoming train. The crossing is also located on a curve, so Rex did not see or hear the train coming. Rex left behind a family, many friends and a lot of memories.

Sexy Rexy the rodeo clown, Sexy Rexy the rodeo clown
Wore only a smile never a frown, he put on a show and never let us down
That was Sexy Rexy, the Rodeo Clown, he had a car name Bullford
He drove it around and chased Gorgeous George, no matter how many times you'd seen it before
Their act would never leave you board. Sexy Rexy you were loved by all
And you never again will take a hit or fall. There will never be a bull on your butt as you crawl
Because now your n Heaven having a ball. We will miss you here on the ground
It will be weird not having you around, I know where you will be found
You are high in the sky and glory bound, You will be missed an loved by all of us.
—Shelly Miller

K.O. HUFF

Kenny Huff—or just K.O., as he was known all his life—was a good example of what this author calls "one of the last old-time cowboys." But that description is a bit misleading. K.O. was born in a dugout in Oklahoma Territory and with his family eked out a living in a true frontier style.

Farming, ranching and trading in order to make a living was a full-time job. Growing up, his father decided to buy his first automobile, loaded up the family and headed to Alva. K.O. was twelve years old at the time and had never driven a car in his life. His father told him to drive it home. He did, but it was not easy.

This set the tone for his whole life. K.O. did what he had to do to make a living and get by. K.O. ended up farming eight hundred acres near Selman, Oklahoma, which is east of Buffalo in Harper County. K.O. and his dad would go to the salt flats, load wagons full of salt and take them to Protection, Kansas, to sell and trade. Protection was the nearest town with a railroad at the time. K.O. bought, sold and traded whatever he could make a dollar on. As a boy, he and his brother, who was two years older, would wire skunks out of their dens and sold the pelts to Sears & Roebuck, as well as any other pelts from animals they managed to trap and skin.

K.O. married Susie Snow, whose father was a doctor in poor health. He thought that moving to the remote area near Selman would let him lighten up his practice. But once people found out that there was a doctor nearby, he was soon as busy as ever. Dr. Snow died young, and K.O. found himself with a wife, three daughters and a mother-in-law he thought the world of. As times were getting harder in the 1920s and early 1930s, he decided to move to Protection and farm. While there, he worked at the local Standard Gas station and continued to trade.

For a time, K.O. went to California and did whatever he could to make a living. His brother had preceded him out there, and K.O. found a job making orange marmalade. When asked if he knew how to make marmalade, he said yes and learned real fast.

K.O. was a mechanically minded man, and if there was something that he needed for the farm, he would build it. Either he could not afford to buy one that was manufactured or there was none available. He always said, "If you needed something, you build it." Of the many inventions that K.O. created to make life easier, he never applied for a patent or tried to start a company to produce any of his inventions.

While living at Protection, he designed a cattle chute that he parked at the local gas station. If anyone needed to use it, they just hooked up to it and brought it back when they were finished. If it needed repairs while it was being used, they would repair it and bring it back. A man decided that the chute was a good idea and started to manufacture one similar to it in Protection, and the company is still there today. The only money K.O. made from it was when he retired back to Protection and worked part-time for the same company.

K.O. took some Ford truck parts and some Baldwin combines and made a self-propelled combine. With it he cut his wheat and custom-cut in Oklahoma and around Protection. The machine's last known location was in a tree row in the Oklahoma Panhandle.

In the 1950s drought, K.O. was in the hay business. He bought, sold and hauled hay. The author's family became friends of K.O.'s at this time. In 1973, when K.O. was seventy-two years old, he came to Wichita and bought some old combines and trucks, and with his grandsons went to Oklahoma and custom-cut wheat. He cut all a man's wheat without a breakdown, and the farmer was so impressed he bought the whole outfit; K.O. came home. It was his last big adventure.

K.O. lived his life in Protection. A book could be written on just his life. One of his grandsons is mural and crop artist Stan Herd. All of K.O.'s grandchildren are very talented.

STUART MOSSMAN: MOSSMAN GUITARS

If you are a bluegrass musician or accomplished guitar player, the name Mossman is familiar. Stuart had roots in the Winfield community but was born in Hinsdale, Illinois, on May 13, 1942. His parents were in education, and his grandfather was president of Cowley County Community College for many years. Stuart would come and spend summers in Winfield as a youth.

Stuart started to work for the Gibson Guitar Company in Michigan, where he learned the art of being a luthier. His opinion, which became his passion, was that the construction of instruments was trading quality for quantity. The practice of using plywood in the construction of instruments was a point of contention for him. Moving to Winfield, Stuart knew that he could build a better-quality guitar for the true musician and started to experiment with designs. He started building guitars in his garage. Stuart's wife was teaching in the schools, and when someone needed or wanted an instrument, he required front money to buy the materials. He also supported himself by giving guitar lessons.

When creating his design, Stuart went to one of the best players in the country for his opinion on his guitar. He gave Doc Watson the prototype to play, and Doc gave him his opinions on improvements. Going back to his garage, he added the suggestions to the design and took the result back to Doc. Doc's opinion was that it was "the second best guitar I ever played."

The process of creating the Mossman guitar began with nylon strings. Stuart spent years in design and built 4,050 prototypes. The guitar he took to Doc was his first steel string model. He asked for Doc's honest opinion, and he got it.

In 1970, Stuart moved guitar building operations to Strother Field outside Winfield, and the S.L. Mossman Guitar Company started commercially building guitars by hand with old-world techniques, the best woods and his proprietary bracing structure. Mossman personally felt that the boom in folk music was creating a huge demand for instruments and that large companies were going more to Pacific Rim countries to produce low-end guitars. Stuart did not like the use of plywood and in one official company statement stated "that after much consideration and discussion they had determined that plywood was excellent wood for concrete forms but they insisted on hardwood in the construction of a Mossman."

In 1975, there was a disaster when a fire in the finishing area resulted in the loss of the building and its entire supply of rare Brazilian rosewood. Fortunately, they were able to rebuild. The company took pride in the quality of the work done. Each instrument was signed by the maker and inspected by Stuart personally. But in an effort to recover from the fire, a deal was made with C.G. Conn Company for a distribution deal—1,200 guitars were produced and sent to Conn's distribution warehouse in Nevada. The problem was that the warehouse was not adequately heated or humidity controlled. This caused surface checking on the Mossman instruments from the baking days and freezing nights and resulted in cracks and breaks. A lawsuit followed when Conn withheld payment for instruments delivered. The resulting legal time, expense and marketing of the checked instruments (the checking did not affect performance) slowed sales.

Layoffs came, and the company never fully recovered. Also, the production of synthesizers and electric guitars cut into the acoustic guitar market. The company struggled, and Stuart's health took a downturn after developing respiratory problems from years of exposure to sawdust and lacquer fumes. The company was put up for sale. A longtime employee, Scott Baxendale, offered to buy inventory, materials and the name. Employees were offered twenty-five instruments made from existing parts before turning over the company. These have become legend. Stuart was a founding member of the Walnut Valley Bluegrass Festival at Winfield.

Stuart appeared in the movie *Cloud Dancer* with David Carradine (1980). A documentary about Stuart was directed by Barry Brown and premiered in the Twenty-Fifth Santa Barbara International Film Festival in February 2010. Brothers Keith, David and Bobby Carradine were huge fans of Mossman guitars and became good friends with Stuart. Others who have played Mossman guitars are Eric Clapton, John Denver, Albert Lee, Doc Wilson, Hank Snow, Cat Stevens, Merle Travis, Dan Crary and Emmylou Harris.

JESSE WILLIAM SHIELDS: INVENTOR

Jesse was born near Holton, Kansas, and became a research pioneer for the Goodrich Tire Company. The use of pneumatic tires on tractors was the focus of experiments. Aircraft tires would not work, as they would slip on the rims. Aircraft and automobiles did not generate the power that a tractor did. The use of pneumatic tires would be a great improvement over steel, especially in soft ground conditions.

He brought the new tire he was testing to Ransom, Kansas, to do the experiments. The ground was soft and was an excellent test of how a pneumatic tire would work. He started with high air pressure, and the results were not good. He dropped the pressure steadily from the eighty pounds he started at to twelve pounds, with added weight for traction that he needed.

The farm he tested at belonged to the Tanners. The Tanners were related to Jesse and, as a side note, were part of the Tanner family to which *Wichita Eagle* reporter Beccy Tanner belongs. Officials came from the Firestone factory to assist and witness the testing. Jesse holds additional patents for weighted and unweighted tractor wheels and other developments for the Firestone Company.

Jesse was born on July 19, 1887, near Holton. He went to Ottawa University, graduating in 1910. He completed his graduate work at the University of Chicago. In 1919, he moved to Akron, Ohio, and went to work in tire design for the Goodyear Tire & Rubber Company. He was coaxed to move over to the Firestone Tire & Rubber Company, where he worked for fifteen years. In 1926, he became sales engineer for the Firestone Company.

Before World War II, he was a consultant for the army and navy. He transferred over to the Firestone War Products Division and designed many items for trucks and tanks. He worked on floats and rubber tracks for tanks. He also designed the Shields Bullet Hole Repair Unit that all army trucks were equipped with, as well as the rubber seals for heavy artillery and shock padding for tanks.

Jesse died in 1965 in Wilmington, Delaware. *Time* magazine called him "one of the US rubber industry's most inventive engineers." Although you cannot say that the tractor tire was invented in Kansas, its designer was born here, and the tests that made the invention successful happened in Kansas.

JOSEPH FIDLER WALSH

Joseph Walsh was born in Wichita, son of Robert Newton Fidler. Joe's mother was a classically trained pianist of Scottish and German ancestry. Joe was adopted by his stepfather at age five after his father was killed in an airplane crash. It was customary in the 1950s to take the name of the stepfather for Social Security, school and health records. Therefore, he took his father's name Fidler as his middle name.

His family moved to Columbus, Ohio, for several years during his youth. At age twelve, the family moved to New York City and then on to Montclair, New Jersey. Joe played the oboe in the school band. Inspired by the success of the Beatles, he replaced Bruce Hoffman as bass player in a local group called the Nomads. He went to Kent State University, playing in various local groups around the Cleveland area. He recorded with the Measles at Super K Productions, Ohio Express.

His music career moved on: the Measles, 1968–71; James Gang, 1971–73; and Barnstorm, 1975–80. In 1975, he was invited to move to England and replace Peter Frampton in Humble Pie. Instead, Joe replaced Bernie Leadon in the Eagles. His first release with the group was "Hotel California," which became the signature song for the group and that group's fifth album. There was some hesitation when adding Joe to the group because he was thought to be too wild. The album's title track topped the charts and would remain the "Holy Grail" of the group to duplicate the success.

The song "Hotel California" contained a guitar duet with Joe and Don Felder, with the vocals featuring Don Henley. *Rolling Stone* magazine placed the guitar duet track on the list of best guitar solos of all time at no. 54. *Guitarist Magazine* also placed the performance in the top solo track of all time.

From 1973 to the present, Joe Walsh has played as a solo artist as well as with a wide variety of musicians; he's also done a lot of studio work. For a short time, he traveled with Ringo Starr. As a member of the Eagles, he won five Grammys and was inducted into the Rock & Roll Hall of Fame in 1998. He was inducted into the Vocal Group Hall of Fame in 2001.

Through all this time, he still maintained connections to Wichita. He even donated the family home near the Wichita State University campus to a nonprofit.

KANSAS (THE BAND)

Kansas is an American rock band that was popular in the 1970s. Its hit singles include "Carry On Wayward Son" and "Dust in the Wind." The band has produced eight gold albums and three sextuple-platinum albums. *Dust in the Wind* was a million-selling album and topped the *Billboard* charts for more than two hundred weeks. Through the 1970s and 1980s, the band sold out venues throughout North America, Europe and Japan. "Carry On Wayward Son" was the second-most-played track on classic rock radio in 1995 and no. 1 in 1997.

In 1969, Lynn Meredith, Don Martin, Dan Wright and Kerry Livgren were performing in a band called the Reason Why in their hometown of Topeka. After changing the band's name to Saratoga, they added Meredith and Joel Warne, Monterey White and Larry Baker. This group lasted until 1971 and then merged with members of a rival band, White Clover. When Erhard, Hope and others left the band to reform White Clover, other various members were recruited. When receiving a recording contract from Don Kirshner's eponymous label, they added members from two other bands, unofficially known as Kansas 1 and 2. The name Kansas became permanent.

The album *Leftovertures* was the group's fourth album and became its breakout album. From 1980 to 1984, members started to drift apart. The band was reunited in 2000 with mostly original members. Through many incarnations and tours with contemporary artists and groups and many differences, Steve Walsh retired on September 1, 2015.

The group signed with Inside Out Music, a German label, and announced that it was working on an album for release in 2016. So, Kansas lives on.

BIBLIOGRAPHY

The Arkansas River

Anything Arkansas. http://anythingarkansas.com/arkepedia.
Cimarron, Kansas. http://www.cimarronkansas.net.
U.S. Territorial Map, 1820. http://xroads.virginia.edu.

The First Buffalo Bill

Kansapedia. "William E. Mathewson." Kansas Historical Society.
Kansas Historical Society. http://www.kshs.org/search/index/query: Mathewson.
Legends of Kansas. "William Mathewson—The Other Buffalo Bill." http://www.legendsofkansas.com/Williammathewson.html.
Woodman, Rea. *Wichitana*. N.p.: self-published, n.d.

Stafford County Short Notes

Stafford County History, 1870–1970. With permission from the Stafford County Historical Museum.

Bibliography

Just Bill: Out of the Frying Pan and Into the Movies

Reflections 19, no. 2 (November 2001).
Stafford County Historical Museum, Stafford, Kansas.
Story written by Michael Hathaway, reproduced with permission.

Exodusters

Stafford County Historical Museum. "The Exodusters." http://museum.staffordcounty.org/Exodusters.html.
Stafford County History, 1870–1970. With permission from the Stafford County Historical Museum.
Tanner, Beccy. "Exodusters." *Kansas Scenic Byways.* http://www.kansaswetlandsandwildlifescenicbyway.com/vimages/shared/vnews/stories/5318d5beda10d/Exodusters%20Brochure.pdf.

Locust Plague: Grasshopper Falls

City of Valley Falls, Kansas. http://valleyfalls.org/our-Town/history.
Kansas and Its Surnames. http://kansasoakland.blogspot.com/2013/01/grasshopper-falls-sautrell-falls-and.html.
Kansas State Historical Society. "Grasshopper Falls." https://www.kshs.org/geog/geog_postoffices/search/placename:Grasshopper%20Falls.

Castleton Movie Set

Bickel, Amy. "Dead Towns of Central and Western Kansas." Kansas Ghost Towns. http://kansasghosttowns.blogspot.com/2010/12/castleton-ks.html.
Center for Kansas Studies, Washburn University. "Kansas in the Movies: Castleton." www.washburn.edu/reference/cks/mapping/movies/mapfilmed/index.html.
YouTube. "1952 Hutchinson Parade for Movie 'Wait Till the Sun Shines Nellie.'" https://www.youtube.com/watch?v=q9WOFDxjl-s.

Bibliography

Skyscrapers of the Plains

Bickel, Amy. "The Prairie Skyscraper." *Hutchinson News*. http://www.hutchnews.com/cbc8e968-2b12-5c11-81f1-44fccc356f85.html.
Grainnet. http://www.grainnet.com.
Hutchinson Kansas Archives, Reno County Historical Museum.
Our Grandfathers' Elevators. "Conversation with Sherman Johnson, Scion of Johnson Construction, of Salina, Kansas." https://ourgrandfathersgrainelevators.com.
Wishart, David J. *Encyclopedia of the Great Plains*. Lincoln: University of Nebraska Press, 2004.

Threshing Machine Canyon

Archives of the Church of Latter-day Saints, Church History Library. https://history.lds.org/article/general_historical?lang=eng.
City of Wakeeney information page. http://www.tregocountyks.com/2268/City-of-WaKeeney.
Kansas Department of Wildlife, Parks & Tourism. http://ksoutdoors.com.
Kansas State Historical Society.
Ransford, Howard, president of the Kansas State Historical Society.
Salina Journal. July 14, 1965; February 2, 1969.

Sellers Motor Car Company

Automobile Manufacturers Worldwide Registry. Jefferson, NC: McFarland & Company: 2000, 251.
Bailey, Marion W. 1909–10 photos of Sellers automobiles and advertisement. Kansas State Historical Society.
Gazette Globe (Kansas City, KS). January 4, 1912, 5.
Hutchinson Commercial Club. "Hutchinson, the Salt City: In the Heart of the Great Kansas Wheat Belt." N.p.: News Printers, 1908, 57.
Hutchinson News. June 11, 1910, 13, advertisement.
Kansas State Fairgrounds, Hutchinson, Kansas. http://winfield.50megs.com/Hutch_Nationals/Fair/18Sep1909.htm.
Ledeboer, Lynn. Reno County Historical Museum.
United States Patent Office. Motor-Tractor, US 1012458 A, Harry C. Shoemaker.

BIBLIOGRAPHY

Engine 252: Orient Railroad

American Locomotives in Histories Photographs, 1858–1949. Mineola, NY: Dover Publications, n.d.
Great Plains Dispatcher. "Looking Back." April 2012, 3.
Joplin Globe. "Mexican Troops Pursue Dynamiters of Train." February 17, 1929, 2.
Kansas State Historical Society. Former Orient engines. http://www.kshs.org/archives.
———. "F Unit 252 Heads Up Freight Train at Summit, CA, Cajon Pass." http://www.kshs.org/archives/51573.
———. "The Santa Fe Locomotive #2509." http://www.kshs.org/archives/61744, http://www.kshs.org/archives/6125.
Newell, Chas. B., "Aid for Orient Railroad in Old Mexico Is Nearer, Shouse Is Getting Results." *Wichita Beacon*, February 13, 1921, 5.
Newspapers.com. https://www.newspapers.com/image. Articles from newspapers.
OK Today 26, no. 4 (Autumn 1976): 6.
Wichita Beacon. "Engines 151 and 252." February 13, 1921; June 4, 1922, 8.
Wichita Daily Eagle. "After a 'Vacation' of 15 Years Mexico Returns Engine." March 5, 1922, 4.
Wiedel, Joe. "Kansas City, Mexico & Orient Railway Company." Receivership Report (ATS&F Board), vol. 3, no. 1. Chicago, Illinois, 1940.
WSU Special Collections. "Tihen Notes." Orient Engine 252. *Wichita Eagle*, February 27, 1922, 7; November 13, 1922, 3.

Richardson Manufacturing

Belleville Telescope. "Beloit Farm Equipment Industry to Expand, Reopen Cawker City Plant." December 31, 1987, 11.
Cawker City Ledger. 1881–1949. Cawker City Museum Archives.
Cawker City Museum. "Richardson Manufacturing Remembered." 1881–2008 archives.
Richardson, Steve, grandson, director of Cawker City Historical Museum.
3I Show 26, issue 1. "Robert Richardson Remembered" (April 2008).

Bibliography

Hines Combine

Chilton Tractor Journal 6 (June 1, 1921): 40.
Farm Show Magazine 24, no. 6 (n.d.): 22.
Hutchinson News. "Daddy of Combines." July 21, 1920; July 2, 1927; September 15, 1996.
———. "Hines Combine Will Expand." July 2, 1927, 14.
Implement and Tractor 37, no. 2 (n.d.): 15.
Letters from Hines customers.
Newspapers.com. https://www.newspapers.com/image.
Spearville News. June 1, 1920; June 21, 1920; August 5, 1920; July 14, 1927.
Successful Farming. "Ageless Iron" (March 2000): 48.
Taylor, Robert. Laverne, Oklahoma. Photos, Hines owner and collector.
Thompson, Douglas. "Not So Tired Iron." *Kinsley Graphic*, July 14, 1994, editorial page.
Trenkamp, Dorthy and Vickie Scheve. Spearville, Kansas. Interview, ephemera and photos.
United States Patent Office, no. 1726667. Combined Harvesters and Thrashers, Michael J. Hines and Allen Webber.

Jacob Wiens Buller: Buller Manufacturing

Beattie, David. Collector/historian.
Berg, Susan. "Buller Company Artifacts Are on Display Downtown." *Hillsboro Star-Journal*, June 18, 2009. http://starj.com.
Clarke, Bascom Byron. "Safety First." *Tractor and Gas Engine Review* 16 (1923): 6.
Gustav, Reimer. Buller family, 1953. www.gameo.com.
Lincoln Star. "Buller Coupler Co., Hillsboro, Kansas." February 16, 1927, 9.
Litke, Virgil. *A Journey with My Grandfather, Jacob W. Buller*. Marion, KS, 1986.
Mennonite Weekly Review. "Buller, Jacob W. (1869–1946)." Obituary, March 28, 1946, 1.
1951 Buller Tractor Mounted Saw Frame, eBay ad.
Stuhr Museum of the Prairie Pioneer's Steam Engine Tractors. http://2014-stuhr-steam-engines.blogspot.com.
Yesterday's Tractors. "Saw Identification–Buller." http://www.yesterdaystractors.com.

BIBLIOGRAPHY

Threshing Stones

Adrian, Jack. Interview with family.
Ediger, Glen. *Leaving No Threshing Stone Unturned*. N.p.: self-published, 2012. https://www.amazon.ca/Leave-No-Threshing-Stone-Unturned/dp/0615682014.
Inman Museum. www.inmanmuseum.com.
Internet Archives. "History of the Threshing Stone." February 21, 2014. https://web.archive.org/web/20140221073956/http://www.threshingstone.com/History.php.
Kaufman Museum. "Threshing Stone: Mennonite Artifact & Icon." Exhibit, Bethel College, North Newton, Kansas.
Mennonite Heritage and Agricultural Museum, Goessel, Kansas.

Max Blue: Blue Star Boats

Blue Star advertisement. I Boats Forum. http://boatsport.org.
BlueStarBoats. https://www.facebook.com/Vintage-Blue-Star-Boat-412605608875187.
Boat Sport Marina. http://www.boatsport.com.
John's Old Mercury Site. http://www.johnsoldmercurysite.com/phpBB3/viewtopic.php?f=15&t=12611.
Joplin Globe. http://newspaperarchive.com/us/missouri/joplin/joplin-globe/1960/04-17/page-6.
Jordan, Patricia. Interview.
Jordan, Robin. Interview.
Lietha, Ronald. Wisconsin/Blue Star collector and restorer.
Newspapers.com. http://www.newspapers.com.
Resourceful Oklahoma 4, no. 6 (June 1953). Oklahoma Planning and Resources Board.
Ternes, Lynda.

Goddard Snake Pit

Goddard, Kansas. "History." http://www.goddardkansas.us/History.
Hosey, Virginia (Mrs. Dale). Interview.

Bibliography

Cero's Candy

Cero, Ed. *Candymakers: A Story of Cero's of Wichita, Kansas, with Recipes.* Morgan Hill, CA: BookStand Publishing, 2012.
Cero's Candies. http://www.ceroscandies.com.
CNN iReport. "Candymakers: A Story of Cero's of Wichita, Kansas." April 22, 2013. http://ireport.cnn.com/docs/DOC-962397.
Neil, Denise. "Dining with Denise: Cero's Candies Has New Owners." *Wichita Eagle*, December 16, 2015.
Wichita Beacon. "Christmas Candies." December 20, 1897.
———. "Tihen Notes." December 20, 1897.

Dr. Samuel J. Crumbine

Averill, Thomas Fox. "Kansas: The Flyswatter State." Political Mavens. http://politicalmavens.com/index.php/2006/11/18/kansas-the-flyswatter-state.
Crumbine, Samuel J., and Frank H. Rose. "The Invention of the Fly Swatter." University of Virginia. http://exhibits.hsl.virginia.edu/insects/swatter.
Grout, Pam. "Sho Fly Don't Bother Me." *Kansas Curiosities: Quirky Characters, Roadside Oddities and Other.* Guilford, CT: Rowman and Littlefield, 2010.
Kansapedia. "Crumbine, Samuel J." Kansas Historical Society. https://www.kshs.org/kansapedia/topic/people.
Reeves, Hope. "Who Made that Fly Swatter?" *New York Times*, May 25, 2012.

J.A. Hockett: Hockett Sterling Tractor

American Society of Mechanical Engineers. "Hart Parr Tractor's Contribution to the Advancement of Agriculture." May 18, 1896. http://docplayer.net/21766513-The-hart-parr-tractor.html.
Charter Gas Engine Company, Sterling, Illinois. http://www.smokestak.com.
Farm Implement News. Advertisement, 1895.
——— 14. "Tractors" (1893): 24. University of Chicago Press.
Hockett Tractor. http://www.wisaconsinhistory.org/records/images/IM96671.
McCormick–International Harvester, photographic collection.

BIBLIOGRAPHY

Robertson, Patrick. "The First Tractor, Agricultural." *Robertson's Book of Firsts*. N.p., n.d.
United States Patent Office no. 559,030. Gasoline Traction Engine, James A. Hockett of Sterling, Kansas, April 28, 1896.
Wendel, C.H. *Gas Engine Magazine*. http://www.gasenginemagazine.com/equipment/reflections-may-1991-1 May/June 1991.
———. *Standard Catalog of Farm Tractors, 1890–1980*.

Barnett Hassocks

Cawker City Ledger. Collection from 1947 to 1973.
Cawker City Museum, Steve Richardson, director. Photos and stories from collection.
Great Bend Tribune. April 18, 1966, 4.
Roberts Family Funeral Service. "Obituary, Edward Barnett." www.mcdonaldrobertsfuneralservice.com/obituary/332600.

McPherson Wetlands

Emporia State University. "McPherson Valley Wetlands." http://academic.emporia.edur/aberjame/student/uttinger2/mvw.html.
Inman Museum. www.inmanmuseum.com.
Kansas Department of Wildlife, Parks & Tourism. "McPherson Valley Wetlands Wildlife Area." http://ksoutdoors.com/KDWPT-Info/Locations/Wildlife-Areas/South-Central/McPherson-Valley-Wetlands.
Queal, Leland. Documents.
Schrag, Rynnell R. "Draining the Big Basin." 1991.

Ogden Publications: Mother Earth News

Cappers Weekly (Topeka, KS). 1913–86. Library of Congress, Humanities Chronicling America.
Kansas Historical Society, Oscar Stauffer and Arthur Capper.
"Ogden Publications. "A Brief History." http://www.ogdenpubs.com.
Teller, Jean. "As American as Mom, Apple Pie & Grit." GRIT. https://www.grit.com/grit-history.

BIBLIOGRAPHY

Topeka Capital-Journal. "Mother Earth News Fair Features Sustainable Living Demonstrations, Workshops." http://cjonline.com.../mother-earth-news-fair-features-sustainable-living-demonstrations-workshops.

Frank Ferguson: Automobile Thresher

Belleville Daily Freeman. 1905.
Belleville History Museum. Copies of copies of photographs.
Bellville Library.
Belleville Telescope. "Automobile Thresher Goes to Kansas City." January 12, 1906. https://www.newspapers.com/newspage/112155761.
———. "The Crossroads Garage." March 27, 1986, 14.
———. "Ferguson's Remarkable Invention." November 24, 1905. https://www.newspapers.com/newspage/112110631.
———. "First Combine May Have Brought About by Early Design of First Automobile Thresher." January 8, 1981. https://www.newspapers.com/newspage/11516944.
———. "A Look at the Past." May 4, 2010. https://www.thebelleville telescope.com/articles/2010/05/04/look-post.
———. "Mechanic Frank Ferguson Was City's Ingenious Inventor of Today's Combine." July 3, 1969. https://www.newspapers.com/newspage/13099421.
Frances, Phyllis Ferguson, Frank Ferguson's granddaughter.
The Horseless Age 18, no. 18 (n.d.): 534.
Stock Certificate for the Ferguson Manufacturing Company, $100. Issued September 20, 1906.
United States Patent Office no. US 998764 A. Drive-gear for motor-cars, July 25, 1911.

Colby Plow Boy Tractor: Jones Manufacturing

Jones Manufacturing, Colby Plowboy Tractor. *Standard Catalog of Farm Tractors, 1890–1980.*
Prairie Drummer (Colby, KS). February 20, 1965.
Prairie Museum of Art and History, Colby, Kansas. Chris Griffin, director. Photos.

BIBLIOGRAPHY

Waconda Springs

Buchanan, Rex, Robert Sawin and Wayne Lebsack. "Water of the Most Excellent Kind: Historic Springs in Kansas." *Kansas History: A Journal of the Central Plains*. N.p., 2000.
Foth, Victoria. *Water and the Making of Kansas*. "Healing Waters: Legends of Lost Waconda Springs." Kansas Natural Resource Council, 1988 and 2010.
Kansapedia. "Waconda Springs." Kansas State Historical Society. http://www.kshs.org/kansapedia/waconda-springs/16720.
Kelly, Matt. "The Great Spirit of Water of Waconda Springs: Mitchell County, Kansas, 1884–1964." *Lost Kansas Communities*.

Royer Tractors

Berry, Mike. "Tilling History." *Wichita Eagle*, November 21, 2004.
Chilton Tractor Journal 4 (1920): 38. https://books.google.com/books?id=d2k4AQAAMAAJ.
Farm Machinery and Hardware. N.p.: Midland Publishing Company, 1920.
Farm Machinery/Farm Power-Gas Engine 21 (n.d.): 297.
Hoffman, Ray. *Antique Power Magazine* (January/February 2005): 42.
Huffman, Julie. Jerry's daughter.
InternetArchives. "Royer." https://archive.org/stream/tractorfieldbook00unse_djvu.txt.
Old Iron Magazine.
Royer sales brochure.
Tractor and Gas Engine Review 13 (n.d.).
Wendel, C.H. *Standard Catalog of Farm Tractors, 1890–1980*. 2nd ed. N.p., 1980, 628.
Wheatland Poppin Johnnies.
Yesterday's Tractors. Discussions forums re: Royer. www.yesterdaystractors.com.

Tyler

Johnson, June. Neighborhood newsletter.
Memories of author and family.

Bibliography

Memories of Cathy Brady and Frank Maus.
Tyler Coop certificate.
Wichita Beacon. July 16, 1919. https://www.newspapers.com/newspage/78389490.
———. 1903.

John David Jordan: Freeport

Anthony City Library Collection.
Anthony Republican/Freeport News. June 18, 1953; June 25, 1953; July 16, 1953; August 20, 1953; August 27, 1953; September 10, 1953.
Boat Sport Marina. "Jordan–Blue Star Boats." http://www.boatsport.com-John.
Coady, Pat. Interview.
Emporia Gazette. October 18, 1947, 1.
Freeport News. 1953, multiple articles.
John's Old Mercury Site. http://johnsoldmercurysite.com/portal/index.html.
Jordan, Pat. Interview.
Kilpatrick Funeral Homes. "Obituary, John David Jordan." June 11, 2015. http://ww.kilpatrickfuneralhomes.com.
Lietha, Ronald, Blue Star boat collector.

Rockefeller Ranch: Frank Rockefeller

American Journal of Science.
Bickel, Amy. "Beautiful Town, Colorful Past." *Hutchinson News*, November 2, 2013. www.hutchnews.com/article/20131102/News/311029879.
Harmon, Terry H. "Soldier Creek Park: The Rockefeller Ranch in Kiowa County Kansas." *Kansas City Posse, the Westerners.* N.p., 1968. www.worldcat.org/title/soldier-creek-park-the-rockefeller-ranch-in-kiowa-county-ks/oclc/8666179.
Kansas State Historical Society. "Edwards County, Kansas History." http://geneologytrails.com/kan/edwards/cityofkinsley.html.
———. "Facet, Kansas Memory." www.kshs.org/km/view/facets:4064,3848,183/sidebar.
Kiowa County Signal. "Did You Know About the Other Rockefeller?" www.kiowacountysignal.com/article/20120704/news/307049979.

Laude, G.A. *Kansas Shorthorns: A History of the Breed in the State from 1857 to 1920*. Iola, KS: Laude Publishing Company, 1921.
Rawlins County-Rootsweb. "Dewey-Berry Feud." http://www.newsarch.rootsweb.com/th/read/Dewey/2004/1078064517.
Rootsweb. http://www.rootsweb.ancestry.com/~ksbarber/belvedere/html.

Ralph K. Odor: Vornado Airplane / Vornado

Daily Capital News (Jefferson City, MO).
Miami Daily News-Record.
Oklahoma Historical Society.
Siebenmark, Jerry. *Wichita Eagle.*
Smith, Dan. Revival of the Coolest. http://www.eichlernetwork.com.
United States Patent Office.
Vornado LLC.
Vornado Trust, Don Morris.

Ace Aircraft Company: Kansas Legacy

Ace Aircraft. "Corbin Sport Planes." http://aceaircraft.com.
Corbin Sport Plane Museum. http://www.aceaidcraft.org/1930.htm.
House, Walt. Wichita Aeronautical Historic Association.
Western North Carolina Air Museum.
Wichita Eagle. "Tihen Notes." Wichita State University Special Collections, March 31, 1930, 1.
Wisconsin Aviation Hall of Fame, Orland George Corben HOF induction.

Dead Cow International

Commemorative Air Force, Jayhawk Wing. http://www.cafjayhawks.org.
McMillin, Molly. "A Conversation with Earl Long." *Wichita Eagle*, May 5, 2013.

Bibliography

Kansas Sunflower

Kansapedia. "Sunflower." Kansas State Historical Society. http://www.kshs.org/kansapedia/sunflower/16899.

Kansas Sunflower Commission. http://www.kssunflower.com.

ProFlowers. "Kansas State Flower, The Sunflower." https://www.proflowers.com/blog/kansas-state-flower-the-sunflower.

State Symbols USA. "Kansas State Flower/Native Sunflower." https://statesymbolsusa.org/symbol-official-item/kansas/state-flower/sunflower.

Hammtown: Norman Hamm

Chilson, Morgan. *Topeka Capital-Journal*, October 23, 2005. http://cjonline/102305/33443_270.jpg.

Ramey, David. "Founder Knew 'Right Is Right.'" *Lawrence Journal-World*, August 6, 2003. http://www2.ljworld.com/news/2003/aug/06/hamm_cos_founder.

Sundown Trail Blog. https://sundowntrailblog.com/tag/hammtown.

The Fleagle Gang

Bickle, Amy. "Betrayed by a Fingerprint—Kansas' Fleegle Gang." *Hutchinson News*, January 29, 2016. http://www.kansasagland.com/news/stateagnews/betrayed-by-a-fingerprint-kansas-fleegle-gang/article_5219274e-1777-5ac5-bcea-da890f92d3b8.html.

Billings, Bud. "Fate of the Fleagle Gang." Victor Records.

Council Grove Republican. "Bandit Car Here." June 8, 1926, 1.

———. March 3, 1921, 1; March 3, 1926, 1; March 5, 1926, 1; October 14, 1930, 1.

Hooper, Mary. "Fingerprint Undoes the Fleagle Gang." *The Legend: Life in Southwestern Kansas* (Fall 2011).

Van Buskirk, Kathleen. "Outlaw for My Neighbor: The Jake Fleagle Story." *White River Valley Historical Quarterly* 7, no. 1 (Fall 1979).

Weiser, Kathy. *Legends of America* (November 2015).

BIBLIOGRAPHY

Robbery at Farmers & Drovers Bank

Council Grove Republican. "Bandit Car Here." June 8, 1926, 1.
———. March 3, 1921, 1; March 5, 1926, 1; June 8, 1926, 1.
Doty, Derrick. "If These Walls Could Talk." From the Barber's Chair. https://fromthebarberchair.wordpress.com/2013/02/13/if-these-walls-could-talk.
Legends of America. "Kansas Legends Robbery at Farmers & Drovers Bank" (n.d.).
McClintock, Ken. Council Grove, Kansas.

Bank Association Vigilantes

Beemer, Rod. *Notorious Kansas Bank Heists.* Charleston, SC: Arcadia Publishing, 2015.
Belleville Telescope. July 23, 1987.
Emporia Gazette. "Vigilantes Go on Range." September 12, 1927.
Garden of the Plain, 1884–1984. Garden Plain Centennial Committee, n.d.
Garden Plain Tribune. February 18, 1921.
Indiana Magazine of History 102, no. 3 (September 2006).
Kansas Genealogy Trails. "Kansas Famous Outlaws." http://genealogytrails.com/kan/famousoutlaws1.html.
Wilgoren, Jodi. *New York Times*, March 31, 2002. www.sfgate.com/crime/article/Big-time-crime-in-middle-America-Bank-robberies-2859138.php.

Edward "Eddie" Adams: Bank Robber

Emporia Gazette. "Claim Prisoner was Adams Pal." February 11, 1922, 1.
———. "Couldn't Find Cache." November 30, 1921, 1.
Garden of the Plain, 1884–1984. Garden Plain Centennial Committee, n.d.
Hutchinson News. "Adams Gang Pulled Moundridge Robbery." November 30, 1921, 7.
———. "Eddie Adams Was Turner Hold Up." November 23, 1921, 13.
———. "Kansas Genealogy Trails: Eddie Adams Admitted Robbing Cullison Store." March 16, 1921, 1.
———. "Members of Adams Gang Are in Jail." November 23, 1921, 1.

Iola Daily Register. "Bandit Eddie Adams Will Be Laid in Grave with Money Found on Him." December 1, 1921, 4.
Scandia Journal. "Kill the Pal of Eddie Adams." December 15, 1921, 8.

Naturalist Camps

Cagey, A.M. "Camp for Nude Witches Fights Closing." Reuters, November 28, 2001.
Hendricks, Mike. "Free Republic." *Kansas City Star*, October 8, 2001.
Lake Edun Foundation. http://www.lakeedun.com.
Prairie Haven. http://www.prairiehaven.com.
Sandy Lane Club. http://www.sandylaneclub.com.

Carl S. ("Stan the Man") Engdahl

American Motorcyclist 12, no. 10. "Everett and Mann Winn Dodge City Features" (October 1958): 28–31.
Kansas Motorcycle Museum. http://www.ksmotorcyclemuseum.org.
National Fallen Firefighters Foundation. http://www.firehero.org/contact.
Quested, Lisa. "Stan the Man." *Eye on Kansas*, June 27, 2007. http://www.eyeonkansas.org/scentral/mcpherson/0701stan.html.

The Runnymede Hotel

Ghost Town. "Runnymede." http://www.gohosttowns.com/states/ks/runnymede.html.
Harper County, Kansas History. http://genealogytrails.com/kan/harper/history1.html.
Harper County Genealogical Society—Kansas Council. http://www.kcgs.us/county-resources/harper-county.
Harper County Historical Society.
Kansapedia. "Runnymede, Harper County." Kansas State Historical Society. http://www.kshs.org/kansapedia/runnymede-harper-county/12187.
OkieLegacy."Alva's Runnymede Hotel Legacy." http://pbpartnersllc.org/woods/alva/alva6.html.
Runnymede Hotel. http://www.therunnymede.com/history_kansas.html.

Bibliography

Rudolph Wendelin: Smokey the Bear

Ancestry.com. "Rudolf Wendelin, Born 1909." https://www.ancestry.com/geneology/records/rudolph-wendelin.

Kansapedia. "Rawlins County, Kansas." Kansas State Historical Society. https://www.kshs.org/research.../inventory-rudolph-wendelinpapers-1930-2005.

Los Angeles Times. "Rudolf Wendelin, Smoky the Bear's 'Caretaker.'" September 4, 2000, obituary. http://articles.latimes.com/2000/sep/04/local/me-15210.

Pearson, Richard. "Rudolph Wendelin Dies at Age 90." *Washington Post*, obituary, September 3, 2000. https://www.washingtonpost.org/wiki/rudy_wendelin.

Rural Kansas Tourism. "Atwood Exploration: Rudolf Wendelin Historical Mural." http://www.getruralkansas.com/Atwood/232Explore/1361.shtml.

Sierra Club. "Rudolph Wendelin: Designer of the 1964 John Muir Commemorative Postage Stamp." http://vault.sierraclub.org/john_muir_exhibit/stamps/rudolph_wendelin.aspx.

Special Collections. "Only You Can Prevent Wildfires." https://specialcollections.nal.usda.gov/guide-collections/us-forest-service-smokey-bear-collection/only-you-can-prevent-wildfires.

McLain's Roundup Rodeo: Sun City

Barber County History Committee. *The Chosen Land: A History of Barber County, Kansas.* Medicine Lodge, KS. Out of print.

Barber County Index. "McLain's Round-Up, Sun City, Kansas, July 8-9-10." June 25, 1938. http://www.rootsweb.ancestry.com/~ksbarber/mclains_roundup_1938.html.

Boot Hill Museum. "Marion McLain, Cowboy Entertainer." http://boothill.org/marion-mclain-cowboy-entertainer.

Brenda McLain, daughter-in-law (Max).

McLain Rodeo Archive. Photos by Homer Venters.

Spencer, Dick, III. "Vintage Rodeo Photographer." *Western Horseman Magazine* (July 1972): 50.

Stories heard at Buster's Saloon and other watering holes.

Bibliography

Orville Brown: World Champion Wrestler

Antiques Roadshow, PBS. "Orville Brown Wrestling Archive, ca. 1940." http://www.pbs.org/wgbh.../21/orville-brown-wrestling-archive-ca-1940--201603W11.

Barber County History Committee. *The Chosen Land: A History of Barber County, Kansas.* Medicine Lodge, KS. Out of print.

Legacy of Wrestling. "Orville Brown Wrestling History." http://www.legacyofwrestling.com/Orville Brown.html.

Online World of Wrestling. "Orville Brown." http://www.onlineworldofwrestling.com/bios/o/orville-brown.

Pro-Wrestling Historical Society. "Orville Brown Biography." http://www.prowrestlinghistoricalsociety.com/brown-orville.html.

Pro-Wrestling Title Histories. "Orville Brown." http://www.wrestling-titles.com/personalities/brown_orville/bio.html.

Wrestling Data. "Richard Brown." http://wrestlingdata.com/index.php?befehl=bio&wrestler=17278.

Yohe, Steve. "Orville Brown Biography." Pro-Wrestling Title Histories. http://www.wrestling-titles.com/personalities/brown_orville/bio.html.

Toad Plague

Kansas Department of Wildlife, Parks and Tourism.
Los Angeles Herald. June 26, 1901.
McPherson Daily Republican. June 29, 1901, 1.

Last Execution in Sedgwick County Jail

Death Penalty USA. "Executions in Kansas, 1853–1965." http://deathpenaltyusa.org/usa1/state/Kansas.htm.

Genealogy Trails. "Sedgwick County Kansas Murders and Mysteries." http://genealogytrails.com/kan/Sedgwick/murdermysteryindex.html.

Harman, S.W. *Hell on the Border: He Hanged Eighty-Eight Men.* N.p.: Phoenix Publishing Company, 1898.

Kansas City Times. September 15, 1888.

Oklahombres. "Execution of the Tobler Brothers, Wichita, Kansas." http://oklahombres.org/eve/forums/a/tpc/f/5176036794/m/43610120021.

Bibliography

Wichita Beacon. "Iron Eyes Saw Two Men Hanged." June 8, 1912, 8, col. 1. https://www.newspapers.com/newspage/76864793.

———. "Tihen Notes." 1888. http://specialcollections.wichita.edu/collections/local_history/tihen/pdf/beacon/Beac1888.pdf.

Wichita Eagle. "Trap Sprung." November 23, 1888, 8, col. 1. https://www.newspapers.com/newspage/62513708.

Wilson, R. Michael. *Legal Executions of Nebraska, Kansas, and Oklahoma, Including the Indian Nations: A Comprehensive Registry.* Jefferson, NC: McFarland & Company, 2012.

Emma Chase: Sue Smith

Smith, Sue. Interview.

Wichita Eagle. "Carrie Rengers." October 16, 2004.

Wilson, Ann. Tallgrass String Band.

Wilson, Ron. Huck Boyd National Institute for Rural Development, Kansas State University.

Kansans Invent Bulldozer

American Profile. "Jim Cummings Patented the Nation's First Bulldozer." December 14, 2003. http://americanprofile.com/articles/jim-cummings-patented-the-nations-first-bulldozer.

Cummings, James, and J. Earl McLeod. "Kansas Legends Biography: The Bulldozer." Legends Outlets, Kansas City. www.legendsshopping.com.

Durst, Duane. Photos, stories and builder of replica bulldozer at Morrowville.

Grout, Pam. *Kansas Curiosities: Quirky Characters, Roadside Oddities and Other.* Guilford, CT: Rowman and Littlefield, 2010.

Penner, Marci. Kansas Sampler Foundation. http://www.kansassampler.org.

United States Patent Office no. US 1522378 A. Attachments for tractors, January 26, 1925.

Working Man. "A Short History of Bulldozers." the-working-man.com/history-bulldozers.html.

BIBLIOGRAPHY

Jim Farrell

Jim Farrell Studios. http://www.jimfsyudios.com/about.html.
Walnut Valley Festival. https://wvfest.com/artists/diamond-w-wranglers.
Wilson, Ron. "Kansas Profile—Now That's Rural." Huck Boyd Institute, Kansas State University, Manhattan, Kansas.

Buffalo Jones: Charles Jesse Jones

Finney County Historical Museum.
History Research Shenanigans. "'Buffalo' Jones: The Man Who Tried to Lasso an Elephant." December 1, 2014.
Jones, Charles Jesse. *Buffalo Jones: 40 Years of Adventure*. Originally printed in 1899. Reprint, Charleston, NC: Nabu Press, 2010.
———. 1996 inductee, Osborne County Hall of Fame.
Kansas Historical Society. Information regarding Charles Jesse "Buffalo" Jones.

Wantha Davis: Jockey

Austin American-Statesman. September 21, 2012.
Cowgirl Hall of Fame & Museum. "Wantha Davis." http://www.cowgirl.net/portfolios/wantha-davis.
Girl Jockey. "Wantha Davis." http://www.girljockey.com.
Rural Messenger. "Roger's View from the Hills." May 17, 2014. http://www.ruralmessenger.com/category/blogs/ringer-ringer-blogs.

Margaret Ann McKenzie: Wichita Carriage Works

Blacksmith & Wheelwright. "Managed by a Woman" (January 1916): 16.
Heaton, Byron. Obituary for Leo McKenzie. *Wichita Eagle,* January 1977.
Kansas State Historical Society.
Leo L. Body Works. *US Cities Directory/Wichita Kansas.* 1937, 1941, 1942, 1946, 1948, 1953, 1955, 1957, 1959, 1961 and 1963.
Maxton, Mike. Find A Grave Memorial.
Old Cowtown Museum, Wichita, Kansas. http://www.oldcowtown.org.

Wichita Beacon. Carriage Works advertisement, June 20, 1903, 7.
———. "Large Works." March 25, 1887, 1; February 12, 1886, 1.
———. "Sam's Auto Stage Gives Real Service." February 12, 1921, 3.
———. "Tihen Notes." Wichita State University Special Collections. Subject: McKenzie.
———. "West Side Bus Line." October 2, 1922, 2.
———. Wichita Carriage Factory advertisement, August 5, 1885, 1.
———. "The Wichita Carriage Works." November 18, 1886, 4.
Wichita Carriage Works, photo. https://www.kansas.com/news/local/w0ti13/picture27884644.
Wichita Daily Eagle. "McKenzie Made Vehicles in Wichita in Pioneer Days." September 24, 1922, 74.
———. "Wichita Carriage Works." September 25, 1921, 56.
Wichita Sedgwick County Historical Museum, photographs.

Sydia Wirt Spreckles: Kansas Turkish Princess

Ancestry.com. Sydia Wirt Spreckles. https://www.ancestry.com.
El Paso Herald-Post. "Sugar Heir Cut in Plane Crash." February 25, 1938, 2.
El Paso-Post. "Sugar Heiress Will Go to Ex-Mate If He Needs Her." February 25, 1938, 2.
Emporia Gazette. "Kansas Girl, Now Turkish Princess, Wins Court Battle." November 1, 1928, 8.
Escanaba Daily Press. "Sidi Is Blushing Bride Four Times." December 8, 1929, 1.
Evening Telegram (Garden City, KS). Local news column, August 27, 1908.
Fort Worth Library, Librarian Suzanne Fritz.
Fuller Foundation. http://www.fullerfoundation.org/GillianSpreckles.
Garden City Herald. "Ed Wirt Dead." September 18, 1913.
Garden City Telegram. "E.L. Wirt Died Last Sunday in Seattle." September 16, 1913.
Hutchinson News. "Sidi Wirt Is Wed to Wealthy Nobleman at Constantinople." July 26, 1923, 9.
Joplin Globe (Joplin, MO). "Princess Seeks Divorce." February 17, 1929, 2.
Kansas City Kansan. "Ex-Chorus Girl–Widow Wins Riches for Baby and Is Granted $20,000." April 27, 1922, 10.
Los Angeles Herald. "Spreckles Jr. and Miss Wirt Married." September 16, 1925 (California Digital Newspaper Collection).
New York Times. "Sues on Spreckles Pearls." June 22, 1922, no page listed.

Bibliography

Newspapers.com. Multiple articles. http://www.newspapers.com.

Oakland Tribune. "Spreckles Rich: No Millionaire; Estate Dwindles." August 18, 1921, 5.

Pasadena Independent. "Engaged—Lord Charles Spencer Churchill" (photo and caption). April 28, 1965, 42.

Reading Times (Reading, PA). "Former Princess Chakir Becomes Bride of Young Army Aviator." December 9, 1929, 4.

Sacramento Union. "Nothing Left for Spreckles' Heirs." November 11, 1921. California Digital Newspaper Collection, no. 25804.

San Bernardino Sun. "One-Time Kansas Farm Girl, Now Turkish Princess, Gets Satisfaction, After Insults." November 2, 1926, 3.

San Francisco Chronicle. "Prince Ali Kamal-Fahmy Bey, Who Was Found Dead Outside His Luxurious Suite in a London Hotel, the Victim of His Wife's Revolver." September 23, 1923, 2.

———. "The Ranch Girls Risk in Marrying an Oriental Prince." September 23, 1923, 2.

Santa Anna Register. "Spreckles' Father to Administer Estate." August 18, 1921, 7.

South Bend New-Times. "Spreckles to Wed Cattleman's Daughter." September 3, 1919, 14.

Tarrant County, Texas, Death Records. June 1, 1970.

Texas Bureau of Vital Statistics, Department of Health. Death Certificate, file no. 45087.

United States Social Security Death Index. Sydia Spreckles, Family Search. The Church of Jesus Christ of Latter-day Saints.

Wichita Daily Eagle. "Tossed Coin to Choose Between Love and Title." September 13, 1921, 1.

Wilmington Morning Star. "Arraign Arbuckle on a Charge of Murder." September 13, 1921, 1.

Wirt and Spreckles Family, Finney County Historical Society.

Utopia College

Babson College. http://www.babson.edu, https://www3.babson.edu/About/History.cfm.

Davidson, Jeff. Eureka, Kansas.

Greenwood County Historical Museum. http://www.gwhistory.com.

Utopia College. https://www.atlasobscura.com/places/utopia-college.

Bibliography

Indian Charley

Biographical Directory of the United States Congress. http://bioguide.congress.gov/scripts/biodisplay.pl?index=c001008.
Cherokee One Feather. "Charles Curtis: America's Indian Vice President." https://theonefeather.com/2014/02/charles-curtis-americas-indian-vice-president.
Curtis, Charles. http://www.vpcharlescurtis.net.
Kansapedia. "Curtis, Charles." Kansas State Historical Society. https://www.kshs.org/kansapedia/topic/people.
National Public Radio. "Curtis, Hoover's VP, Touted Mixed Race Heritage." www.npr.org/templates/story/story.php?storyId=92301413.
Native American Netroots. "American Indian Biography." http://nativeamericannetroots.net/diary/642.
United States Senate. "U.S. Senate: Charles Curtis, 31st Vice President (1929–1933)." https://www.senate.gov/artandhistory/history/common.../VP_Charles_Curtis.htm.
Washington Post. "Herbert Hoover's Vice President, Charles Curtis." https://www.washingtonpost.com.../herbert-hoovers-vice-president-charles-curtis-was.

America's First Patented Helicopter

Connecticut History. http://www.connecticuthistory.org.
Edison Nation. "America's First Patented Helicopter." https://www.edisonnation.com.../americas-first-patented-helicopter-and-the-reason-i-a.
Goodland, Sherman County, Kansas. "America's First Patented Helicopter" http://www.visitgoodland.com/tag/americas-first-patented-helicopter.
High Plains Museum. "Helicopter." http://www.highplainsmuseum.org/tag/helicopter.
Kansapedia. Kansas State Historical Society.
Kansas Tourism. "America's First Patented Helicopter." https://www.travelks.com/listing/americas-first-patemted-helicopter/2924.
Purvis, Joseph, great-nephew of William Purvis. Edison International. http://www.edison.com.
Rural Kansas Tourism. http://getruralkansas.org; https://www.getruralkansas.com/goodland/210Explore/1807.shtml.
Stingray's Rotarcraft Forum. http://126840.activeboard.com/+44242921/Purvis-wilsons-1909-goodland-helicopter-americas-first-rotar.

Mayrath

Hutchinson/Mayrath Company History. http://www.hutchinson-mayrath.com/about-us.
Kansas GenWeb and Kansas Historical Society. http://www.ksgenweb.org/Mayrath.
Lawn and Garden Tractor Forums. http://gardentractortalk.com/forums.
Mayrath Lawn Tractor History. http://www.tractordata.com/lawn-tractors/tractor-brands/mayrath/mayrath-lawn-tractors.html.

Duane Nelson: Cowboy

American Cowboy Magazine. "Ken Spurgeon" (September/October 1994).
———. "Roger Ringer" (May/June 1998).
Biglow Funeral Directors. "Duane Nelson." http://www.biglowfuneraldirectors.com/memsol.cgi?user_id=1505129.
Bisel, Debra Goodrich. *Kansas Music: Stories of a Rich Tradition.* Charleston, SC: The History Press, 2014.
Information drawn from the memories of the author.
Kansas African American Museum. *Images of America: African Americans of Wichita.* Charleston, SC: Arcadia Publishing, 2015.
News OK. "History of Black Cowboys to be Topic." http://newsok.com/article/2756267.
Wondra, Keith, and Barb Myers. *Old Cowtown Museum.* Charleston, SC: Arcadia Publishing, 2016.

Teresa Cuevas: Mariachi Estrella de Topeka

Chicago Times Tribune. "Extrodinary People We Lost in 2013: Teresa Cuevas—Matriarch and Musician." CNN iReport, January 23, 2014.
Dingham, Alex. "34 Years Ago Today, KC Walkway Collapse Killed over 100." WIBW, July 17, 2015.
Historical Marker Database. "Mariachi Divina!" https://www.hmdb.org.
Kansas Humanities Council—Grants Justica Inc. "Mariachi Estrella: Ad Astra Per Aspera" (14,792).
Laessig, Gavon. "Mariachi Divina: New Film Celebrates Legacy of Kansas Mariachi Legends, Mariachi Estrella de Topeka." *Lawrence Journal World,*

February 20, 2010. http://www2.ljworld.com/news/2010/feb/20/mariachi-divina-new-film-celebrates-legacy-kansas-.
Topeka Capital-Journal. "Mariachi Estrella de Topeka–We Remember." July 24, 2001. http://cjonline.com/stories/072401/opi_mariache.shtml.

Lawrin: Kentucky Derby Winner

American Hereford Journal. September 1, 1916.
Doolittle, Bill. "Eddie Arcaro." The Kentucky Derby. https://www.kyderbybook.com/pages/learn-more-132.
Joseph, Dr. Steven, Kansas City Veterinary Medical Association (KCVMA) historian. "Stout Heart at the Finish." May 7, 1938. http://www.kcvma.com.
Kentucky Derby. "2006: Barbaro." http://www.kentuckyderby.com/2006/derby_history/derby_charts/years/1938.html.
Mission Road Antique Mall. http://www.MissionRoadAntiqueMall.com.
Missouri Valley Special Collections.
Thoroughbred Heritage. "Lawrin's Grave." http://www.tbheritage.com/TurfHallmarks/Graves/cem/Grave MattersWoolford.html.
Time. "Man on a Horse." Biography of Eddie Arcaro, May 17, 1948.

Hap Peebles: Entertainment Icon

Anthony Kansas Library. Anthony Republican Archives.
Couch, Ernie, and Jason Couch. "The Plainsmen, a History." Ernie Couch & Revival. www.erniecouchandrevival.com/plainsmen.shtml.
Daddy-O Dilly. "Hap Peebles Remembered." June 6, 2009. http://daddyodilly.blogspot.com/2009/06/hap-pebbles-remembered.html.
Entertainment Buyers Association. https://www.ibea.org/about.
Highbeam Business. "Industry Mourns Death of Promoter Hap Peebles." January 18, 1993. https://business.highbeam.com/53/article-1G1-13884872/industry-mourns-death-promoter-hap-peebles.
Information from Harry "Hap" Peebles' family.
Sherrarden, Jim, Elek Harvath and Paul Kingsbury. *Hatch Show Prints: The History of a Great American Poster Shop.* San Francisco, CA: Chronicle Books, 2001.
Wishart, David. *Encyclopedia of the Great Plains.* Lincoln: University of Nebraska Press, 2004.

Sexy Rexy: Rex Allen Pyeatt

Flemming, Theresa. Correspondence.
Leach, Shelda. Sister. Mulvane, Kansas.
Legacy.com. "Rex Allen Pyeatt, Obituary." http://www.legacy.com/obituaries/kansas/obituary.aspx?page=lifestory&pid=184247558.
Memories and poem from Shelly Miller, George Leach and family.

K.O. Huff

Huff, Kenneth O. Comanche County history.
Iola Register. August 22, 1959.
Memories of the Ringer family.
Ringer, Roger. "Life and Times of K.O. Huff, Parts 1, 2 & 3." Cowboy Storytellers Association of the Western Plains newsletter.

Stuart Mossman: Mossman Guitars

Dallas Morning News. "Betty Mossman Obituary." March 18, 2012. http://www.atkinsonfuneralhome.net.
Internet Movie Database. "Stuart Mossman: A Modern Day Stradavari." http://www.imdb.com/title/tt1592882.
New York Times. "Stuart Mossman, 56, Guitar Maker to Stars." March 5, 1999. http://www.nytimes.com/1999/03/05/arts/stuart-mossman-56-guitar-maker-to-stars.html.
Southern, John. "Old Fashioned Craftsmanship: Mossman Guitars." Talking Guitars. http://www.talkinguitars.com/guitar_stories/mossman.html.
Stanley, Deborah. "Bio. of Dr. Frank E. Mossman." Iowa History Special Project. May 14, 2005. http://iagenweb.org/history.
Steadham, Wayne. Interview.
Walnut Valley Festival. http://wvfest.com.

Jesse William Shields: Inventor

New York Times. "Jesse W. Shields, 78 Dies; Invented Tire for Tractors. Radium, Kansas." August 12, 1965.

Bibliography

Tanner, Beccy. "Our Own History: The Great Tire Experiment." Radium, Kansas, 2010. http://radiumkansas.tumblr.com/post/1125930118/our-own-history-the-great-tire-experiment.
———. "Today's Trivia (September 12)." *Wichita Eagle*, August 30, 2011. www.kansas.com.
United States Patent Office, no. 2,123,861. J.W. Shields—Weighted Tractor Wheel, July 12, 1938.
United States Patent Office, no. 2.150,107. J.W. Shields—Tractor Wheel, March 2, 1939.
Wichita Eagle.

Joseph Fidler Walsh

AllMusic. "Joe Walsh, Biography and History." https://www.allmusic.com/artist/joe-walsh-mn0000808214/biography.
ArticleBio. "Joe Walsh Biography." http://articlebio.com/joe-walsh.
Internet Movie Database. "Joe Walsh Biography." http://www.imdb.com/name/nm0909695/bio.
Joe Walsh Online. "Biography." http://www.joewalshonline.com/biographyhtm.
Nysse. "Joe Walsh Anthology." http://www.nysse.com/jw/anthology.html.
Walsh, Joe. "About." https://www.joewalsh.com/about.

Kansas (the Band)

Ankeny, Jason. "Artist Biography." AllMusic. https://www.allmusic.com/artist/kansas-mn0000303626/biography.
Kansas band website. "History." www.kansasband.com/history.php.
Kansas Facebook page. https://www.facebook.com/KansasBand.
Kansas Official Website. http://kansasband.com.
Krammer, Kyle. "Kansas Is America's Band." NOISEY. https://noisey.vice.com.
The Robinson Library. "Kansas." http://www.robinsonlibrary.com/music/groups/kansas.htm.
Songfacts. "Kansas Artistfacts." http://www.songfacts.com/facts-kansas.php.
Wright, Renee. "Kansas Documentary Celebrates 40 Years of Rock." AXS. https://www.axs.com/kansas-documentary-celebrates-40-years-of-rock-37213.

INDEX

A

Abplanalp, Jerry
  Antique Power Magazine 60
  Royer owner and restorer 59
Academy of Western Artists 98
Ace Aircraft Company 69
  Ace Scooter airplane 70
  Baby Ace airplane 70
  Junior Ace airplane 70
  Super Ace prototype plane 70
Adams, Edward "Eddie" (aka William Joseph Wallace) 78, 81, 82
Adams Gang 81
African American Museum 120
Aircraft Welders Company 67
Alaska Gold Rush 100
Alva, Oklahoma 85
American Cowboy Magazine 119
American Legion 83
American Motorcycle Association 83
American Society of Mechanical Engineers Bulletin list of chartering of companies 47
Andover, Kansas 69
Anthony, Kansas 80, 123
Anthony Republican 123
Antique Power Magazine 60
Arbuckle, Rosco "Fatty" 106
Arkansas River 13, 51
Arkansaw Territory 13
Aulne (town) 35
automobile thresher 55

B

Babson College 110
  Midwest Institute of Business Administration 110
Babson, Reverend Roger 110
  "Babson's Magic Circle" 110
  relative Roger W. Babson, burned at the stake in England 111
Baby Ace airplane 70
Back Home Magazine 54
Bailey, Willis, Governor 72
Bangs, Wantha. *See* Davis-Bangs, Wantha

INDEX

bank robberies 75, 77, 78, 79, 80, 81
Barber County, Kansas 87
Barnett, George, and son E.J. (Edward John) 48
Barnett Hassocks 48
  Cawker City Ledger 49
  Hollywood bed ends 49
  Living for Young Homemakers 49
  Saturday Evening Post 49
  Stow Away hassock 48
  vacuum cleaner chests 49
Barton County Arts Council 20
Barton County, Kansas 19
Baxendale, Scott 130
Bazaar, Kansas 27
Becker, Carl 62
Beeler (town) 20
Bellville, Kansas 54
Belvidere (town) 65
Bethel College 39
Billy the Kid 103
Bishop, Pam and Darcy 44
Blacksmith & Wheelwright 104
Blair, Ed, "Ode to the Sunflower" 73
Blendon (town) 41
Blue, Max 40, 42
  collector Ronald Lietha of Wisconsin 41
Blue Star Boats 40, 42
Boeing Wichita 71
Borton LLC 23
Bowman, Officer Charles 82
Broom Weed Festival 94
Brown, John 19
Brown, Orville 88

Buffalo Jones: 40 Years of Adventure 101
Buffalo Pitt Company 57
Buffalo Rider (movie) 101
Buhler High School 39
Buller, Jacob Wiens 35
  American Thresherman 36
  Buller Coupler 36
  Case Tractors 37
  forerunner of the motor home 36
  obituary, *Mennonite Weekly Review* 37
  snap coupler hitch 35
  Thresherman's Review 36
Buller Manufacturing Company 37
  Buller saws 37
  full-vision tractor cab 37
  Hesston Corporation 37
  LP gas conversion kits 37
  Montgomery Ward Catalogue 37
  sawblade setting tools 37
Bultaco Motorcycles 64
Bureau of Investigation 76
Bureau of Reclamation 58

C

Camp Gaea, near McLouth 83
cane syrup 16
Cannonball Green 41
Capper, Arthur, and *Grit Magazine* 54
Carver, George Washington 20
Case Tractors 37
Casner, Officer Ray 82
Castleton (town) 21
  Castleton movie set 21

Index

20th Century Fox 21
   Jean Peters and David Wayne 21
   Wait 'til the Sun Shines, Nellie 21
Caterpillar bulldozer 94
Catherine the Great 39, 51
cattalo (Buffalo Jones) 101
Cawker City Historical Museum 32
Cawker City, Kansas 29, 48
Cedar Bluffs Reservoir 24
Cero, Peter 43
Cero's Candy 43
   Albrecht family 44
   Bishop, Pam and Darcy 44
   Mental Health Association of South Central Kansas 44
Chase County Courthouse 93
Chase, Emma 93
Cheney, Kansas 80
Cherry Creek Gold Rush 23
Cheyenne Bottoms 50
Cheyenne County, Kansas 65
Cheyenne Wyoming Frontier Days Rodeo 126
Chief White Plume (Kaw) 111
Chosen Land, The 86
Churchill Downs 101
Churchman, Dale 42
Civil War 19
clutch, invention of 54
Coady, Milford and Pat 64
Cody, William F. "Buffalo Bill" 14, 98
Colby Plow Boy Tractor 56
Colorado 14
Columbus XVII (bull) 65
Comanche County, Kansas 33
Conway, Kansas 50

Corben, Orland George 69
Corben Sport Plane Company 70
Cottonwood Falls, Kansas 93
Country Music Association 124
Cowboy Heritage Festival, Dodge City 120
Cowgirl Hall of Fame 103
Cowley County, Kansas 82
crime committed in Indian Territory 91
Croup, Michael 69
Crumbine, Dr. Samuel 45
   American Child Health Association 46
   Autobiography of a Pioneer on the Frontier of Public Health 45
   Crumbine Award 46
   Dixie Cups 45
   "Don't Spit on the Sidewalk" 45
   fly swatters 45
   inspiration for "Doc Adams" on *Gunsmoke* 46
   Kansas State Fair 45
   Rose, Frank, of Weir City, and his Boy Scouts 45
   fly bats 45
   tuberculosis 45
   University of Kansas Medical School 46
Cuevas, Teresa
   first all-female mariachi band in the United States 121
   Hyatt Regency skywalk collapse 121
   Mariachi Estrella de Topeka 121
   Mexican Fiesta 122
      Our Lady of Guadalupe Church, Topeka 122

Index

Cummings bulldozer replica 96
Cummings, James 94
Curtis, Charles, vice-president 114
  Curtis Act of 1898 112
  Curtis, Owen, father 111
Curtis JN4 "Jenny" airplane 69
Curtis, Theresa Permillia "Dolly" 114
Custer, George Armstrong 24

D

Dalton Gang 16
Daughters of the American Revolution 86
Davidson School of Business 97
Davis Act 112
Davis-Bangs, Wantha 101, 103
Davis, Lendol 101
Dead Cow International 70
Delaware River 20
Dewey Berry Feud 66
Dewey, Chancey 66
Diamond W Wranglers 98
Dodge City, Kansas 101, 116
Dodge dealership 30
Dorsey, Dr. J.O. 13
Dumont, Ray 124

E

Economical Five Radio 30
Eco-Village, North Carolina 53
Ediger, Glenn 39
  Leave No Threshing Stone Unturned 39
E.D. Richardson and Sons Mfg. 31
E.D. Richardson, Cawker Machine and Repair Shop 30
Eisenhower (Mid Continent) Airport 71
Ellis County, Kansas 39
El Paso, Texas 109
Emma Chase Café 93
Engdahl, Carl S. ("Stan the Man") 83
Engine no. 252, Pancho Villa attack 28
Erd engine 47, 60
Eureka, Kansas 110
Exodusters 19
Experimental Aircraft Association 70

F

Fairfax, Virginia 107
Farmers & Drovers Bank at Council Grove 77
Farrell, Martha Slater 98
Farrell, Tennessee Jim 96
Federal Court in Wichita 91
Ferguson, Frank 54
  automobile thresher 55
  clutch, invention of 54
  Moline boat engine 56
    Phyllis Ferguson, granddaughter 55
Finney County, Kansas 100
Firestone Tire & Rubber Company 131
First Colored Infantry 19
First Generation Video 98
First Mennonite Church 36
Fish and Wildlife Service 50

INDEX

Fitzpatrick, Officer Robert 82
Fleagle Gang 75, 77, 78
Fleagle, Jake 76, 78
Flexible Combine Pick-Up 31
flooding in Topeka, Lawrence and Kansas City 59
fly swatters 45
Ford County, Kansas 116
Ford Motor Company 56
  patent infringement 56
Fordson tractor 95
Fort Riley, Kansas 79
Fort Sumter 19
Freeport Cemetery 64
Freeport (town) 63
Fullerton, Ernie 119
full-vision tractor cab 37

G

Garden City, Kansas 100
Gardner, Frank 81
ghost towns
  Castleton 21
  Utopia 110
Gist, Pinky, rodeo clown 87
Gleaner Baldwin combines 34
Glenn Elder Dam 58
Goddard, Kansas 40, 41
Goddard Snake Pit 41
  Churchman, Dale 42
  Hosey, Dale and Virginia 42
Goessel (town) 22
Goodland Aviation Company 115
Goodland, Kansas 114
Goodrich Tire Company 131
Goodyear Tire & Rubber Company 131

Grand Canyon 101
Grand Ole Opry 96, 124
Grand Ole Opry Show at the Forum 125
Grasshopper Falls. *See* Valley Falls, Kansas
grasshopper plagues 20
Grasshopper River. *See* Delaware River
"Great American Desert," the 50
Great Depression 31, 34, 70, 78, 89, 114
Great Lakes Navy Band 66
Greensburg well 42
Greenwood County Historical Museum 111
Greenwood County, Kansas 110
Grey, Zane 101
Grim, Charles 16
gyrocopter 115
  U.S. Patent no. 1,028,781 (gyrocopter) 116

H

Hall of Great Western Performers, Cowboy Hall of Fame 98, 101
Hamm, Norman 73
Hamm's Municipal Solid Waste Landfill 74
Hammtown 73
Harper County Historical Society 85
Harper County, Kansas 63, 84
Harper County, Oklahoma 128
Harper, Kansas 85
Hartnew, Oklahoma 101

165

INDEX

Harvey County, Kansas 51
Hawkins-Sheppard wedding 125
Haynes, "Doc" 15
Haynes, Irwin Willis 56
  Colby Plow Boy Tractor 56
helicopter, the first patented in America 114
Herd, Stan, mural and crop artist 129
Hereford Breeders Association 65
Hesston Corporation 37
Hesston, Kansas 34
Hillsboro, Kansas 35
Hines Combine Company 32
  Hines, M.J. 32
  Tony Trenkamp, Spearville 34
Historic Fox Theatre, Hutchinson, Kansas 98
Hockett, J.A. 46
  Erd engine 47
  Gasoline Thresher and Plow Company 46
  gasoline traction engine, patent in 1896 46
  Hockett Sterling Tractor 46
  Sterling traction engine built in Canada 47
Hockett Sterling Tractor
Robertson's Book of Firsts 47
Hoffman, Detective Charles 82
Holly & Sullivan Ranch 106
Home Place Studios 96
Hoover, Herbert 114
Hosey, Dale and Virginia 42
House of Representatives, First District 112
Hoy, Dr. Jim 120
  "Prairie Poetry: Cowboy Verse of Kansas" 120

Huff, Kenny "K.O." 33, 127
  Herd, Stan, mural and crop artist 129
  orange marmalade 128
  self-propelled combine 129
  Snow, Susie 128
Humane Extension Feeder 30
Hutchinson, Kansas 25
Hutchinson Manufacturing Company 118
Hutchinson/Mayrath Company 118
Hyatt Regency skywalk collapse 121
hydroplane boats 63

I

Indian Charley 111. *See* Curtis, Charles
Indian tribes and nations
  Dheigiha 13
  Kanza 13, 58
  Kaw 112
  Kiowa 14
  Omaha 13
  Osage 13, 111
  Pawnee 58
  Ponca 13
  Potawatomi 111
  Quapaw 13
Inman, Kansas 50
Insco, son of Sir Gallahad III 122
International Harvester Company 57
  Case-IH 57

INDEX

J

J-38 Land and Cattle Company 97
James, Frank 76
jamming 94
Jim Farrell Studios 98
Jones, Charles J. "Buffalo" 98
   game warden, Yellowstone National Park 101
Jordan, John David 63
   Dodds, Patricia, wife 63
   friends with Max Blue 40
   Jordan, Patricia 40
   military service 63
Jordan's Saw and Marina 64
Junior Ace airplane 70
Just Bill 16

K

Kansa language 111
Kansas 150, Century II Auditorium 98
Kansas Bureau of Investigation 80
Kansas City Farm Show 60
Kansas City Implement Dealers Show 30
Kansas City, Mexico & Orient (KCM&O) Railroad (aka Orient Railroad) 27
   Santa Fe Railroad 28
Kansas City Monarchs of the Negro American League 124
Kansas Historical Society 27
"Kansas: Home on the Range" 98
Kansas Humanities Council 121
Kansas, Mexico & Orient Railroad 85
Kansas Motorcycle Museum 83
Kansas National Guard 73
Kansas State Agricultural College 29
Kansas State Fair 45
Kansas State University 23, 63
   milling science technology 23
Kansas Territory 14
Kansas (the band) 133
   "Carry On Wayward Son" 133
   "Dust in the Wind" 133
   Inside Out Music, German label 133
   Saratoga (the band) 133
   the Reason Why (the band) 133
   White Clover (the band) 133
Kansas, the Sunflower State 71
Kansas Wildlife, Parks and Tourism 50
Kanza Indians 13, 58
Kaufman Museum 39
Kaw Allotment Act 112
Kaw Reservation 111
Kiowa County, Kansas 64
Koening (German motor company) 64

L

Lafferty, Dave "Prairie Dog" 119
Landon, Alf, presidential campaign 73
Landos, Jim, world wrestling champion 89
Last of the Plainsmen 101
Lawrin, son of Insco 122
   Kentucky Derby winner 122
Leave No Threshing Stone Unturned 39

INDEX

Lillie, Gordon "Pawnee Bill" 98
Lincoln, Abraham, a family friend 100
Litke, Virgil 38
   A Journey with My Grandfather, Jacob W. Buller 38
Little Arkansas River 50
Lloyd's of London 18
Los Angeles Herald 90
LP gas conversion kits 37
luthier 129

M

Macksville Depot 16
M.A. McKenzie Body Works (later the Leo McKenzie Body Works) 104
Mariachi Estrella de Topeka 121
Marion County, Kansas 22, 35, 51
Marquette, Kansas 83
Marriage Combine 33
Marriage helicopter 114
Martin, Frank, State Representative 72
Massey-Harris 33
Maxwell cars 30
Mayrath, Nicholas 116
McCarty, Catherine, mother of Billy the Kid 103
McConnell AFB 71
McCook, Nebraska 100
McKenzie, Daniel and Margaret Ann (Friend) 103
McLain, Marion F. "Mac," rodeo owner and producer 86
McLeod, J. Earl 95
McPherson County, Kansas 51
McPherson Daily Tribune 90
McPherson, Kansas 50, 90
McPherson Rural Fire District No. 2 83
McPherson Wetlands 50, 90
   Conway, Kansas 50
   Inman, Kansas 50
   Little Arkansas River 50
   McPherson, Kansas 50
   Valley Center, Kansas 50
Mechanics Illustrated 70
Medicine Lodge Peace Treaty Pageant 88
Medicine Lodge Treaty 15
"Memories of Tyler" 61
Mennonites 51
   first Mennonite Church 36
   Mennonite Weekly Review 37
   Swiss Volhynian Mennonite communities 39
Mercury Outboard Motors 64
Micheaux, Oscar, black movie producer 19
Middle Tennessee State University 97
Missouri State Prison 81
Mitchell County, Kansas 29
Moline boat engine 56
Montgomery Ward Catalogue 37
Morehouse, George, Senator 72
Morrowville, Kansas 94
Mossman, Stuart 129
   Baxendale, Scott 130
   C.G. Conn Company 130
   Cloud Dancer, movie with David Carradine 130
   Gibson Guitar Company 129
   luthier 129
   Mossman Guitars 129, 131

INDEX

Santa Barbara International Film Festival 130
S.L. Mossman Guitar Company 130
Strother Field 130
Walnut Valley Bluegrass Festival 130
Watson, Doc 129
Mother Earth News 52
  Eco-Village, North Carolina 53
  "Plowboy Interview" 52
  Woods, Bruce, editor 53
motorboat racing 40, 63
  runabouts 40
Mullinville, Kansas 33, 114

N

Nashville Symphony Chorale 96
National and International Pipeline Contractors Association 96
National Buffalo Association Hall of Fame 101
National Cowboy Symposium, Lubbock, Texas 120
National Fallen Firefighters Foundation Roll of Honor 84
National Motorcycle Racing Champion 83
National Wrestling Alliance 90
naturalist camps 82
Negro American League 124
Nelson, Duane 118
  African American Museum 120
  American Cowboy Magazine 119
  Cowboy Heritage Festival, Dodge City 120
  "Cowboys of Color" 118
  Lafferty, Dave "Prairie Dog" 119
  National Cowboy Symposium, Lubbock, Texas 120
  Old Cowtown Museum 118
  sit-in protests at Dockums Drug Store lunch counter 118
New Runnymede, Kansas 85
New York Stock Exchange 21
Nicodemus (town) 19
Ninnescah River, North Fork 21
Norman Hamm Inc. 74
N.R. Hamm Quarry 74
nudist camps 82

O

O.A. Sutton Company 68
Odor, Ralph K. 66, 69
  Morris, Don, grandson 69
Ogden Publications Group
  Mother Earth News 54
Oklahoma 13
Oklahoma A&M University 66
Oklahoma State Fair 17
Oklahoma State Penitentiary 76
Oklahoma State University 66
Oklahoma Territory 112, 127
Old Cannonball (original US Highway 54) 41, 61, 79
  Cannonball Green 41
Old Cowtown Museum 98, 118
Old Iron Magazine 60
Orient Railroad 28
Osborne County Hall of Fame 101
Osborne County, Kansas 100

INDEX

P

Parish, A.N. 76
Parish, J.N. 76
patent infringement 55
Pawnee tribe 58
Peebles, Hap 123
   Country Music Association 124
   Grand Ole Opry Show at the Forum 125
   Hap Peebles Agency, Wichita 126
   Hawkins-Sheppard wedding 125
   International Country Buyers Association (ICBA) 124
   Topeka tornado in 1966 125
   White Chapel Memorial Gardens, Wichita 126
Perry, Oklahoma 100
Perry Reservoir 20
Pike, Lieutenant Zebulon 58
Pioneer Oil Company 65
pneumatic tires 131
Prairie Drummer (Colby) 56
Prairie Fire Festival 94
Prairie Museum of Art and History 56
Prairie PastTimes 94
Prairie Rose Chuckwagon Supper near Benton, Kansas 97
Prairie Rose Wranglers 97
Prairie Village, Kansas 123
Pratt County, Kansas 80
Propellair 67, 68
Protection, Kansas 128
Purvis, William J., first patent for a helicopter 114
Pyeatt, Rex Allen 126
   Bullford, Sexy Rexy's clown car 127
   Cheyenne Wyoming Frontier Days Rodeo 126
   Purdy, Janet 127
   Sexy Rexy, rodeo clown 126

Q

Quarter Horse Hall of Fame 103

R

Ransom, Kansas 131
Rapp, Virginia, actress 106
"Rarin to Go" (song) 87
Rattlesnake Creek 16
Rawlins County, Kansas 65, 86
Reno County, Kansas 21, 33, 51
Reno County Museum 27
Reyher, Fredrick 21
Richardson, Emmit David 29
   Dodge dealership 30
   Economical Five Radio 30
   Maxwell cars 30
Richardson Manufacturing Company 29
   AD-Flex Plow 32
   E.D. Richardson and Sons Mfg. 31
   Flexible Combine Pick-Up 31
   Humane Extension Feeder 30
   Stay Kleen straw walker cover 32
   Sunflower Manufacturing, Beloit 32
Riley County, Kansas 63
Ringer, Lloyd and Erma 62
RKO movie studio 17
Roaring Twenties 78

INDEX

Robertson's Book of Firsts 47
Rockefeller, Franklin "Frank" 65
  Columbus XVII (bull) 65
  Hereford Breeders Association 65
  military service in the Civil War 65
  Seventh Ohio Infantry 65
  Sherman's March to Atlanta 65
Rockefeller, John D. 64
Rockefeller Ranch 66
Roosevelt, President Theodore 101, 122
Royer Ensilage Harvester Company 59
Royer Tractor Company 59
  Royer D 12-25 60
runabouts 40
Runnymede, England 84
Runnymede, English colony 84
Runnymede Hotel 84

S

saltwater spring 58
Santa Fe express train 82
Santa Fe Railroad 21, 28, 51, 61, 65
Saturday Evening Post 49
Schoewe, Walter H. 59
Sedgwick County Fire District No. 1, Station 3 62
Sedgwick County Jail 91
Sedgwick County, Kansas 62
Seiling, Oklahoma 101
Sellers Motor Car Company
  formerly St. Joe Motor Company 25
  Sellers 35 car 25

Seventh Ohio Infantry 65
Seward (town) 19
Sexy Rexy, rodeo clown 126
Sharon, Kansas 90
Sherman's March to Atlanta 65
Shields, Jesse William 131
  Firestone Tire & Rubber Company 131
  Goodrich Tire Company 131
  Goodyear Tire & Rubber Company 131
  Shields Bullet Hole Repair Unit 131
  Tanner Farm 131
  Wichita Eagle reporter Beccy Tanner 131
Shoemaker, Harry
  Motor Tractor, patent 25
Shultz, Charlie, rodeo clown 87
Shuttleworth, John and Jane 52
Sikorsky, Igor, VS-300 helicopter 114
Sinclair Oil Company 94
Singleton, Benjamin "Pap" 19
"skyscrapers of the plains" 22
slip-form construction of elevators 22
Smith, Sue 93
Smokey the Bear 86
Smokey the Bear Project 86
Smokey the Bear stamp 86
Smoky Hill River 51
Smoky Hill Trail 23
snap coupler hitch 35
Soldier Creek Ranch 64
Solomon River 58
Sousa, John Philip 66
Spreckles, Sydia "Sidi" Wirt 105
  Chakir, Prince Suad Bey, of Turkey 107
  El Paso, Texas 109

INDEX

Gardner, Lieutenant Roger 107
Kansas Turkish Princess 105
Rapp, Virginia, actress 106
Spreckles, Geraldine, daughter of Sidi 106
Spreckles, John D., II 106
Wirt, E.L. (Edward), father of Sydia 105
Stafford County Historical Museum 16, 18
Stafford County, Kansas 16
Stafford Courier 18
Standard Catalog of Farm Tractors, 1890–1980 56, 59
Standard Oil Company 65
Starr, Ringo 132
Stauffer, Oscar Stanley 54
Stay Kleen straw walker cover 32
steam traction engine 55
Sterling, Kansas 46
Stipa, Luigi 66
Stipa-Carproni airplane 67
St. Joe Motor Company 25
St. John, John, Governor 19
St. John, Kansas 19
St. Louis World's Fair 58
Stolen Women, starring Janine Turner 120
Stone, Milburn 46
Strother Field 130
Stuckey, D.C. 82
Sun City (town) 86
Sunflower Manufacturing, Beloit 32
Super Ace prototype plane 70
Sutton, O.A. 67, 68
Swiss Volhynian Mennonite communities 39
Symmonds, Brigadier General Charles 79

T

Teapot Dome, Wyoming 94
Texas Agriculture and Mechanical College (Texas A&M University) 96
Thomas County, Kansas 56
Thoroughbred Hall of Fame 103
Threshing Machine Canyon 23
threshing stones 38, 39
  Buhler High School 39
  Kaufman Museum 39
toad plagues 90
Tobler, Jake and Joe, executed 91
Topeka tornado in 1966 125
Trego County Historical Museum 24
Troy, Kansas 100
tuberculosis 45
Turkey Red wheat 22, 39
Turner, Janine, actress 120
Turnly, Edward, founder of Runnymede 84
Two Guys Discount Department Store 68
Tyler Cooperative Company 61
Tyler Road in Wichita 61
Tyler Station 61

U

Ukraine 22, 35, 38, 51
University of Kansas 86, 106
U.S. Department of Agriculture 86
U.S. Department of Defense 96
U.S. Forest Service 86
Utopia College. *See* also Babson College

INDEX

Greenwood County Historical Museum 111
Utopia, Kansas 110
utopian societies 82

V

Valley Center, Kansas 50
Valley Falls, Kansas 20
Valley View Cemetery 101
Venters, Homer, cameraman 87
vigilantes, organization of 79
Volga Catholics 38
Von Tilzer, Harry 21
Vornado Air Circulation Company 69
Vornado airplane 66
  Dodge, Kern 67
  patent application 67
  Propellair 67
  Sutton, O.A. 67
  twin engine 67
  Vornado Trust 67
Vornado Fan 68
  Andover, Kansas 69
  Vornado Air LLC 69
  Vornado Trust 68

W

Waconda Springs 58
  saltwater spring 58
  St. Louis World's Fair 58
  Waconda Flier water 58
Walker, George Washington 19
Wall Street crash of 1929 70
Walnut Valley Bluegrass Festival 130
Walnut Valley Festival 94
Walsh, Joseph Fidler 132
  Frampton, Peter, replaced in Humble Pie 132
  Guitarist Magazine 132
  Leadon, Bernie, replaced in the Eagles 132
  Rock & Roll Hall of Fame 133
  Rolling Stone magazine 132
  Starr, Ringo 132
  Vocal Group Hall of Fame 133
Washington County, Kansas 95
Watson, Doc 129
Wendelin, Rudolf 86
West, Ed, Sheriff 82
Western Heritage Cowboy Hall of Fame 88
Western Music Association 98
Westport Airport 71
wetland areas 51
  Big Basin 51
  Cheyenne Bottoms 50
  McPherson Wetlands 50
  Quivira 50
Wheatland Poppin Johnnies Tractor Club 59
Wichita Beacon 43, 61
Wichita Carriage Works 103
Wichita Eagle 65, 120, 123
Wichita Fire Department, first two hose wagons 104
Wichita Police Department, first paddy wagon 104
Wichita & Western Railroad 61
Winfield, Kansas 101, 129
Woods, Bruce 53
Woolf, Herbert M. 122

INDEX

Woolf Brothers Clothing stores 122
Woolford Farm 122
World War I 33, 60, 66, 69, 78
World War II 31, 43, 48, 61, 67, 68, 86, 96, 116, 131
Wright-Patterson Air Base 67

Y

Yellowstone National Park 101
Young, Brigham 23